how to choose a
FRANCHISE

2nd edition

iain murray

KOGAN PAGE

Publisher's note
Every possible effort has been made to ensure that the information contained in this book is accurate at the time of going to press, and the publishers and author cannot accept responsibility for any errors or omissions, however caused. No responsibility for loss or damage occasioned to any person acting, or refraining from action, as a result of the material in this publication can be accepted by the publisher, the author or Express Newspapers.

For ease of expression only, the male pronoun has generally been used throughout this book.

First published in Great Britain in 2003 by Kogan Page Limited
Second edition 2004

Apart from any fair dealing for the purposes of research or private study, or criticism or review, as permitted under the Copyright, Designs and Patents Act, 1988, this publication may only be reproduced, stored or transmitted, in any form, or by any means, with the prior permission in writing of the publisher, or in the case of reprographic reproduction in accordance with the terms of licences issued by the Copyright Licensing Agency. Enquiries concerning reproduction outside those terms should be sent to the publishers at the undermentioned address:

120 Pentonville Road
London N1 9JN
www.kogan-page.co.uk

© Express Newspapers 2003, 2004

British Library Cataloguing in Publication Data

A CIP record for this book is available from the British Library

ISBN 0 7494 4195 X

Typeset by Saxon Graphics Ltd, Derby
Printed and bound in Great Britain by Thanet Press Ltd, Margate

Contents

	Introduction	1
1.	**For yourself but not by yourself**	5
	The appeal of franchising	5
	Success stories	6
	Franchising defined	8
	The growth and diversity of franchising	11
	Common features of franchises	13
	Types of franchise	14
	Advantages and disadvantages of franchises	16
	Successful franchise relationships	21
2.	**Know yourself as others know you**	23
	Personal strengths and weaknesses	23
	Your self-assessment	26
	The questionnaire	27
	Analysing the results	30
3.	**When all is not what it seems**	37
	Franchise or business opportunity	37
	Choosing a business opportunity	40
4.	**The great franchise myth**	43
	The myth	43
	The debunking	44
	The underlying truths	47
5.	**The search begins**	49
	Narrowing the choice	49
	Where to look	51

Setting your financial targets		55
Calculating your personal net worth		60
Location		60
Setting the ball rolling		61
6.	**Snooping and sleuthing**	**62**
	Investigating the business opportunity	62
	Begin with a broad brush	63
	Investigating the franchise	65
	The franchise interview	65
	Reviewing the situation	68
	Meeting existing franchisees	69
7.	**The crunch: individual investment opportunities**	**73**
	Location, location, location	73
	Buying an existing franchise	76
	Starting afresh	77
	Seeking professional advice	78
	Making the decision: a final checklist	80
8.	**The large print and the small**	**82**
	The franchise contract	82
9.	**Raising the wind**	**92**
	Using a clearing bank	92
	Franchise finance packages	94
	The Small Firms Loan Guarantee Scheme	95
	How to prepare a business plan	96
	Approaching your bank	102
10.	**The ups, downs, and ups again**	**105**
	Your franchise relationship	105
	The ideal franchisor	107
	Individual enterprise	109
11.	**It's a woman thing**	**111**
	Suits you, madam	111
	Success stories	112

Domino's Delivers

In the 44 years that we've been in the pizza delivery business, Domino's Pizza has grown to more than 7,000 stores, delivering over a million pizzas a day in 50 international markets.

Our business strategy - "to safely deliver a hot, freshly made, quality pizza within 30 minutes of taking the order"- couldn't be simpler, yet it says everything about our company, our pizzas and our franchisees.

'Freshly made' means we only use the finest ingredients - fresh (never frozen) dough for our pizza bases, 100% mozzarella cheese, and a sauce made with specially selected Portuguese tomatoes.

Domino's franchisees are passionate about pizzas, their staff and their customers. They guarantee that only quality pizza leave their stores. Domino's delivery areas are specially designed so that our drivers can safely deliver a hot and fresh pizza to our customers.

By sticking to this strategy and by making sure that all our franchisees have the benefit of intensive training and excellent support, Domino's Pizza has become the UK's No.1 pizza delivery company.

If you really want to know what makes Domino's Pizza a cut above the rest, just have one delivered.

If you'd like your own slice of our thriving business, please call the Domino's Franchise Department on 01908 580000.

Alternatively, please visit our web site: www.dominos.co.uk

		Page
	Partnerships	115
	The last word	116
Case studies		**117**
	Domino's Pizza	119
	Kall Kwik	124
	Rainbow International	128
Appendices		**133**
I.	**Understanding company accounts**	**135**
	The balance sheet	135
	The profit and loss statement	137
	The cashflow statement	137
II.	**Selling**	**139**
	Effective sales techniques	139
	Know your product or service	140
	Know your customer	140
	Marketing	140
	Advertising	141
	Cold calling	141
	Practice makes perfect	142
III.	**The British Franchise Association members**	**143**
	Full members	143
	Associate members	157
	Provisional members	165
	Affiliate professional advisers	174
IV.	**Useful Web sites**	**184**
	Index of advertisers	*184*

Franchise opportunities

The following pages contain a selection of available franchise investment opportunities.

earning
not
yearning

Live in the lap of luxury

Owning a Kall Kwik franchise won't always be plain sailing, however with effort and commitment the rewards can be significant. Average Centre sales are among the highest in the sector. Top Centres achieve sales well in excess of £1 million.

With substantial net profits available, a Kall Kwik franchise can deliver the wealth to fulfil your personal ambitions. To find out how you can start living the dream call **0500 872060** or visit our web site www.kallkwik.co.uk

unique opportunities for **unique** individuals

kallkwik
business design + print

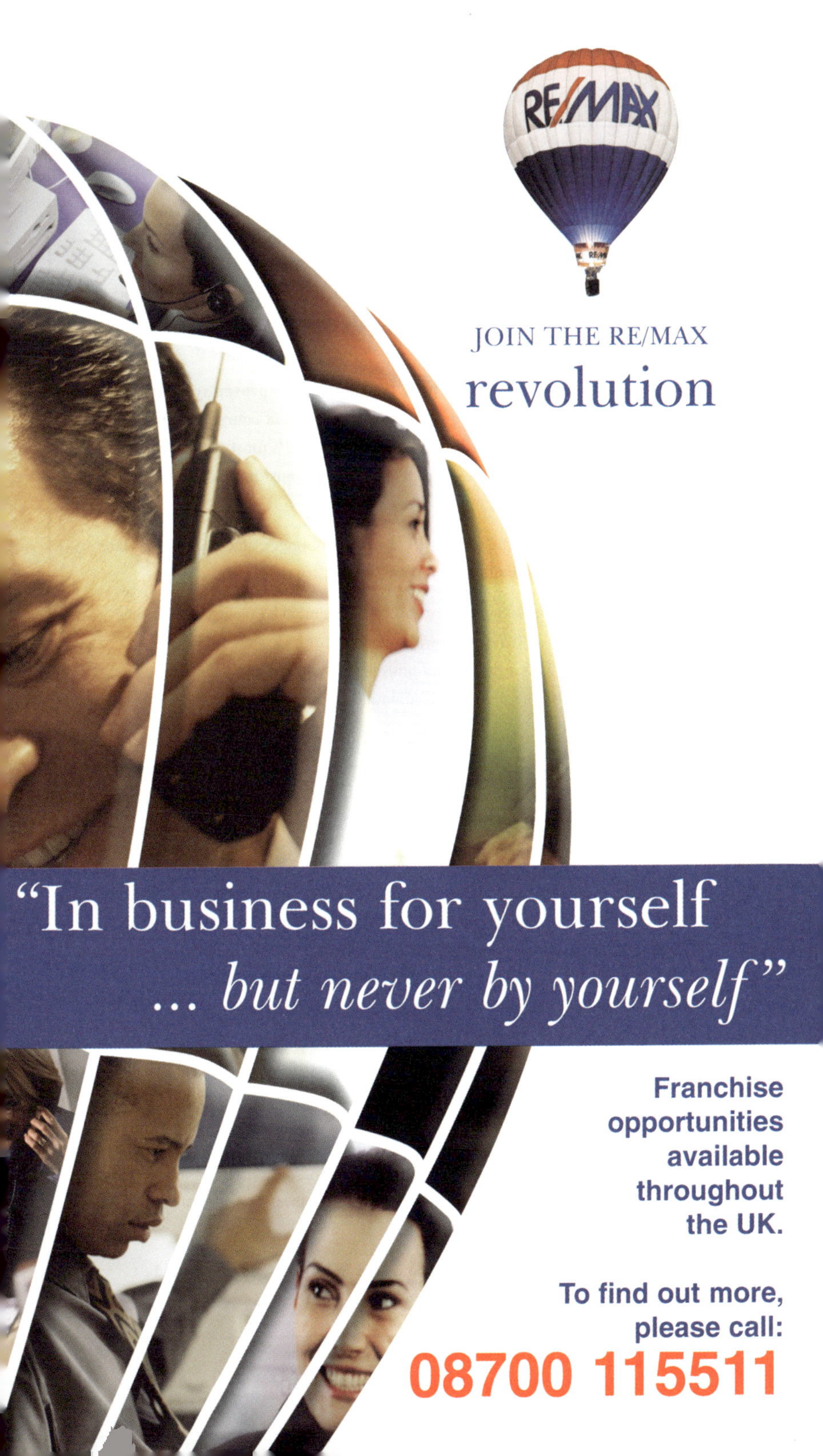

JOIN THE RE/MAX
revolution

> "In business for yourself
> ... *but never by yourself*"

Franchise opportunities available throughout the UK.

To find out more, please call:
08700 115511

"In business for yourself ... *but never by yourself*"

The RE/MAX franchise opportunity is like no other. It genuinely offers the 'best of both worlds' – an independent estate agency business within a major, international organisation.

From day one, franchise owners have the support of a proven system; a huge advantage for anyone planning a new business. And, of course, you're buying into an internationally recognised brand – the world's most successful property marketing business – which creates an almost immediate market presence.

RE/MAX was started in the USA in 1973 by Dave Liniger, an experienced estate agent who had become disillusioned with the industry.

He, like many other good agents, had become frustrated by the limited earning potential and career path available within the industry. He sought to create an alternative way of working – first for himself and now for many thousands of ambitious, hard working individuals around the world.

The system created was designed to recruit and retain top producing negotiators (known in RE/MAX as Sales Associates) by providing a supportive and nurturing environment for them to work in. Their rewards would directly reflect their results. The system was named RE/MAX (REal estate MAXimums), alluding to the prime objective of maximum service for maximum reward.

Since then, RE/MAX has grown to become the most successful estate agency business in the world, with more than 4,500 independently owned and operated offices and 80,000 Associates in 43 countries. By the time you read this, the figures will have risen; in the entire history of RE/MAX, there has never been a period of more than 30 days when the organisation hasn't expanded!

Already well established across Europe, RE/MAX is now becoming a significant force here in the British Isles. By the spring of 2003 there were over one hundred offices open in the UK and Ireland. This figure is projected to rise to a total of 1000 offices nationwide.

The RE/MAX revolution is well and truly here, and with it comes a unique opportunity - the chance to change the way people think about estate agents and property marketing forever.

After all ... can 80,000 RE/MAX Associates and 4,500 Office Owners be wrong? They obviously don't think so!

Who are RE/MAX Office Owners?
The RE/MAX proposition appeals to business people from every area of professional life.

For existing estate agencies, the RE/MAX network provides an opportunity for expansion well beyond anything possible on an independent, local level. For individuals (estate agents or not), it is the chance to start a business with the kudos and marketing advantages of an international brand and the business support of a major organisation, through their regional offices.

The opportunities offered by RE/MAX have also been recognised by IFAs, lawyers, surveyors and other professionals as the ideal way to diversify into a market that is clearly beneficial to their core business. Whether it's mortgage or other financial services, conveyancing etc, the 'one-stop-shop' principle is very attractive to business-owner and customer alike.

And, of course, experienced business people seeking good returns on investment should look seriously at RE/MAX. With the training and support systems RE/MAX offer, previous estate agency experience in not necessary.

What is a RE/MAX Office?
A RE/MAX office is the 'high street' presence – the estate agency showroom – and is owned and operated by the Office (franchise) Owner.

Behind the scenes, the Office provides the infrastructure and administration support for any number of Associates to develop their own RE/MAX property sales business. In turn, rather than having paid employees, the Office Owner will attract independent Sales Associates – a system similar to that used by barristers in chambers.

The RE/MAX system will attract top performing individuals from within the estate agency industry as well as sales people from other fields. The structure encourages the successful to stay within the business, helping the Office become market leaders.

Why franchise with RE/MAX?
New business or established agency re-brand, RE/MAX provides each Office with an immediately recognisable identity, familiar to millions of people throughout the world. The system RE/MAX has developed is effective, cost-efficient, and (perhaps most importantly) thoroughly tried and tested. A franchisee will find it hugely supportive and flexible enough to allow the development of an independent business beneath the umbrella of the global organisation.

Check out the RE/MAX difference for yourself!

◆ **Have you ever** sat in a hospital waiting room and wanted something hot to eat but the restaurant is closed?

◆ **Have you ever** been at work during the night and felt hungry but the restaurant staff have long gone?

◆ **Have you ever** been a student coming home after a night out and had neither the energy or resources to cook?

◆ **Have you ever** checked into a hotel and then realised the restaurant and room service are closed?

◆ **Have you ever been any of these people?**

If the answer is **yes** then you will realise the solution that Hot Bite can provide. An exciting new franchise, Hot Bite provide innovative, first-to-market vending machines including toasted sandwich, panini and pizza options. Products are **not microwaved** but are in fact freshly toasted. Popcorn and muffin options also available.

Snack Point Limited
Southwood Farm
Southwood Road
Alton, Hampshire
GU34 4EB
T: 01420 80230
F: 01420 87562
E: enquiries@hotbite.co.uk
W: www.hotbite.co.uk

Launched in the UK in April 2002 as a franchise operation, Hot Bite was pioneered to fill a gap in the market for vending machines which could provide fresh, non-microwaved hot food 24 hours a day, seven days a week. Indeed, increasingly hectic consumer lifestyles have encouraged a rising trend for convenience food to-go, something which has arguably afforded Hot Bite a niche in the market.

At the outset, Hot Bite's core business was the toasted sandwich vending machine – a revolutionary, first-to-market product that toasts fresh sandwiches between hot plates in a specially sealed bag within 90 seconds. The machine proved to be an immediate success and Hot Bite quickly expanded their range to include new products – panini, pizza, wrap, popcorn and muffin vending options.

Hot Bite is always looking at new developments and concepts that will add value to its franchise and one such concept provides a total food and drink solution. Under the working title of Auto Café, Hot Bite offer a complete food and drink offering through a matrix of selected vending machines complimented by small seating facilities. The Auto Café would essentially negate the need for staffing on site as well as providing a way of reducing costs and providing an alternative meal offering should other facilities be closed. The Auto Café can feature a toasted sandwich, wrap, or panini machine, pizza machine, popcorn, muffin and ice cream options as well as coffee, fresh orange juice, snack and can offerings.

From humble beginnings, the past twelve months have been extremely rewarding for Hot Bite. In fact, the company has franchised out over 30 territories and has more than 150 machines now operating in the UK alone. The machines have been such a national success that they have caught the attention of several major companies including Tesco and South West Trains. Such alliances increase exposure for the franchise and contribute to genuine brand recognition.

At present, Hot Bite is also actively responding to international franchising enquiries. Indeed, the company is in discussion with various interested parties in over 30 countries worldwide from Holland to India to the United States. Negotiations have so far centred on granting either the Master Franchise (essentially a micro version of Hot Bite UK in another country) or exclusive distribution rights (exclusivity to distribute and sell machines in a specified country).

How the Hot Bite franchise works:
The Hot Bite franchise works in a way similar to many other UK franchises. Sole rights are assigned to a specific territory with identifiable potential for the siting of Hot Bite machines, which are leased from the franchisor. Commercially, the franchisee's task is to develop their business within their designated territory both in terms of managing existing sites and finding suitable new outlets. Established market sites for Hot Bite machines include

railway stations, universities, hospitals and call centres; whilst emerging market sites for Hot Bite machines include hotels, theme parks and retail outlets.

From an operational perspective, franchisees need to ensure machines are working efficiently and are well stocked at all times. The Hot Bite franchise can be operated from home, avoiding the overheads of separate business premises, at least to begin with. However, when a franchisee places a number of machines in the marketplace they will be encouraged to utilise a chilled distribution van in accordance with Hot Bite requirements. Importantly, franchisees are not required to prepare any of the food products, which are sourced direct from Hot Bite approved suppliers. For those already established in the catering trade, Hot Bite are pleased to discuss 'own supply' arrangements.

The inclusive key benefits of a franchise with Hot Bite are:
- Unique vending concept (UK & European patent)
- Exclusive territory rights
- Excellent sustainable income
- Access to ongoing new products
- 3 months lease paid on initial 2 machines
- 1 year machine maintenance inclusive

As franchisor, Hot Bite provide a wealth of assistance to help new franchisees. Indeed, Hot Bite provide comprehensive induction training which covers technical and operational aspects of all the Hot Bite machines as well as core sales and marketing training. Another benefit of the Hot Bite franchise is the business launch programme which provides new franchisees with professional PR support. Furthermore, there is a dedicated lead generation support team as well as a business stationery starter pack and point of sale material. Hot Bite also assist with national and regional corporate accounts as well as product development, consumable development and delivery and business planning both financially and legally.

Expected financial benefits:
While individual profits may vary, the expected financial return from a Hot Bite franchise can be very high. For instance, a franchisee operating 20 Hot Bite toasted sandwich machines vending 200 sandwiches a week at £1.80 can look to generate an operating profit of £52,000 pa. Importantly, when the lease period ends after 3 years earnings can increase substantially.

If you are interested in a Hot Bite franchise please do not hesitate to contact the team on:
+44 (0)1420 80230 *or at* **enquiries@hotbite.co.uk**. *Alternatively, visit our website at* **www.hotbite.co.uk**

SprayAway

Picture: Courtesy of Simon Carpenter Foster

GET SMART!

GAIN ACCESS TO:

A unique repair system that covers:

Chips / scratches / bumpers / small bodywork / alloy wheels / windscreens / interior velour, vinyl and leather repairs

The SprayAway Franchise Offers You:

- A huge hig-demand market
- Comprehensive, simple to learn state of the art technology for repairing cars and motorcycles
- Extensive training both on and off site with experienced, senior franchisees acting as 'mentors'
- Full exclusive / protected postal code area for your business
- Ongoing marketing support and technical backup and R & D
- Low cost set-up

For an information pack containing further details on this Franchise, please contact us on

01430 837213

There is a vast, ongoing market for trained professionals who can carry out high quality repairs to minor damage on both cars and motorcycles (including e.g. holes in windscreens, chipped, scratched or dented paintwork, scuffed or split bumpers, damaged motorbike fairings, cigarette burns in seats, carpets and door linings, interior damage to leather, vinyl and plastic material, etc.)

An opportunity to enter into this lucrative market is available to all those who are accepted to become a franchisee in the well established SprayAway network. The SprayAway system contains processes, chemicals and patented equipment that are unique to the franchisor. Furthermore, the extensive training programme is carried out by experienced franchisees, over a four week period, and includes one week of hands-on experience in car dealerships under the tutelage of one of five "mentors", who are available at any time (together with central office staff) for future help and advice. All these measures help ensure that the work carried out by SprayAway franchisees is of the highest quality.

SprayAway see their training, ongoing technical backup, support, marketing and research & development as second to none – all genuine benefits of owning the SprayAway franchise.

Since the Directors of SprayAway own the Parent Company, this keeps the cost of the franchise (and its consumables) at a low value and permits incorporation of any new innovative technology including that resulting from their own Research & Development programme.

These benefits, coupled with the assignment of one Franchisee only to any one post code area, means that SprayAway can, with confidence, guarantee all Franchisees the opportunity to compete effectively in the marketplace where they can expect to be earning easily £30k by the end of their first year of trading and a minimum of £50k by the end of their second year.

Make your move from stalemate to checkmate...

Making the big career decisions takes careful consideration and planning, and without the right knowledge and guidance you could find yourself in a stalemate situation.

By becoming part of a leading franchise in the cleaning and restoration industry, you will benefit from 20 years of experience and expertise in this massive marketplace.

With a Rainbow International franchise, the pieces are perfectly placed for you to make all the right moves, enabling you to develop a long-term winning strategy.

Call Ron Hutton now to find out why Rainbow International is the clever move for you...

01623 675100

www.rainbow-int.co.uk • ron@rainbow-int.co.uk

- Recognised brand
- Free training
- Professional marketing
- National contracts
- Your own area
- Growth opportunities
- National support
- Opportunity for secure retirement

BRITISH FRANCHISE ASSOCIATION FULL MEMBER

- a part of ISS DAMAGE CONTROL

Rainbow International
CARPET CARE & RESTORATION SPECIALIST
- a company in the ISS Group

Build your business on the Internet revolution

"A perfectly packaged, proven B2B franchise opportunity."

At Netspace® UK we help companies build their businesses using internet technology.

The growth is there and the demand is explosive.

So if you…

- Are itching to expand your personal horizons?
- Relish the challenges of being your own boss?
- Recognise the power and potential of the internet as a business opportunity?

…then a Netspace® UK franchise will make perfect sense.

Exclusive territory, full marketing and sales support including appointment setting, and a business franchise model that delivers monthly recurring income - just some of the benefits of being part of the Netspace® UK organisation.

In the US, Netspace® has perfected its range of internet consulting services and e-commerce marketing tools especially for the small to medium sized business sector. And now, the USA's top provider of franchised internet consulting services, is realising its strategic ambitions to be the world's number one
'internet consulting' brand with the appointment of the UK Master Franchisee.

We are now looking for individuals from a variety of commercial backgrounds including sales and marketing, IT and communications, professional and management who want to join us and share our vision.

Above all we are looking for people who recognise the power of the internet, have a desire to help companies build their business using internet technology and who are keen to generate monthly recurring income.

Your next step: contact UK Master Franchisee Shaun Thomson on 0870 7702545 for an informal chat

More information is available on our website: www.netspace-uk.co.uk

" Be part of the Vision"

John Eccles House   Robert Robinson Avenue   Oxford Science Park, Oxford OX4 4GP
T. 0870 7702545   F. 0870 7702546   info@netspace-uk.co.uk   www.netspace-uk.co.uk

Internet Britain Leads Europe – Fact!

With Britain's on-line selling and e-commerce economy topping the magical ONE BILLION pounds per month in November 2002, the e-commerce revolution really has begun to make that big impact on how we shop and the way we do business.

Shaun Thomson, CEO of Netspace® UK sets out some of the myths that persist regarding the Internet.

Myth number 1: *"Large Businesses are best placed to take advantage of the World Wide Web!"*
Reality: The cost of web space is relatively inexpensive, so smaller companies can have a web site as impressive as a Times 200 company.

"The Internet allows smaller companies to compete with the large multinationals in the eyes of the on-line consumers."

"Another way of looking at it," explains Shaun, "is that Netspace® consultant's help small-medium sized businesses take their fair share of that £1billion per month, which people and businesses are spending on-line in the UK. No matter what business they are in, if they do not get their Internet strategy right, they will simply be missing out on this huge potential revenue."

Myth number 2: *"We have a web site and it gives us no benefit!"*
Reality: Having a web presence is only the beginning of using the Internet to build your business. Less than 10% of businesses with a web site have an Internet strategy and, even partially, understand how to use this dynamic medium to help build their businesses.

Shaun explained: "Five years ago we thought everybody would be shopping in 'Virtual Shopping centres' using a computer and never going outside. Thankfully this never happened. What we have discovered is that the Internet is just another channel to connect businesses with their customers, and all the "Old World" rules apply."

The problem is, where do businesses go for advice and fulfilment of all their Internet requirements? Most original websites for small-medium businesses were built by 'Freds in Sheds' who have long disappeared. The poor website owner is left with an out of date site that he does not know how to change and has no measure of the negative impact this is causing his or her business.

Myth number 3 *"The Internet and e-commerce may be happening in America and the rest of the world, but not in the UK!"*

Reality: Wrong. Tony Blair promised that the UK would be the best place in the world to do e-commerce by 2002. A benchmark report by Booz Allen Hamilton put the UK second behind the US and leaders in Europe. In another survey, from Neilsen/Netratings, the UK leads the world in conversion of browsers to shoppers with a staggering 70% conversion rate. The UK's European pole position is also confirmed by consumer spending online in the run up to Christmas - Forrester Research claims that the European market is slightly larger than the American market and that the brightest star in Europe is the UK.

No business can afford to ignore the Internet. If you would like to discuss how Netspace can help you set-up in business to take advantage of the Internet, then contact Shaun Thomson on **0870 770 2545** or email **shaun@netspace-uk.co.uk**

Our philosophy on helping franchisees build their business is unique. We can only be successful if our franchisees are successful. It is our guiding thought when awarding franchise territories and when we help and support franchisees each and every day. Practical, business-growing support is always available to enhance our franchise concept and assist our franchisee build their exclusive territory.

Introduction

Franchising is a growing part of the UK economy. It is a multifarious activity estimated to be worth £10 billion. It can transform lives. And yet it is still not sufficiently appreciated. That, at any rate, is the conclusion of research by the British Franchise Association. Naturally, the association is disappointed that the sector over which it presides is not more widely understood, mainly because greater understanding would mean more recruits and more rapid growth. That said, franchising is unlikely ever to become a dominant force in the economy. That is because not everyone has the ambition, drive and self-belief to leave the calmer waters of paid employment for the turbulence of self-employment.

For those that do, however, franchising has much to offer, not least because it is a kind of half-way house between working for someone else and working for yourself. Through offering a ready-made business format and teaching newcomers from myriad backgrounds how to make it work for them, franchising provides an attractive alternative to the daunting task of coming up with a business idea and launching an enterprise from scratch. Moreover, it can provide a new start in life for people who need it most, people who have perhaps been made redundant or who, for one reason or another, have become deeply dissatisfied with their job and feel their efforts are undervalued, people who perhaps have reached middle age in an economy that values only youth. Franchising can say to these people, 'We can help you, we can train you, we can teach you how to become a restaurateur, a property manager, a dog trainer, a private detective. And we'll always be there to give you encouragement, guidance, and support.'

It's a seductive proposition. But it is not a free ride. Franchising is much harder work than some of the advertisements would have you believe. Yes, the business system you choose should have been tried and tested; yes, you should get training and continuing support; yes, you will be given every chance to succeed. But as with every enterprise, success or failure is ultimately down to you, to your efforts, to your sheer bloody-minded determination to make it work and grow.

In fact, in some ways it is more difficult to be a franchisee than an entrepreneur. When you are wholly self-employed, you call the shots, you make the key decisions, you shape the future of a business that is yours in every sense. Franchising is not quite like that. To be a successful franchisee – or indeed to be a franchisee at all – you must adopt other people's ideas, follow their way of doing things, and stick more or less rigidly to the tried and tested systems that attracted you to the idea in the first place. That can be okay to begin with, but once you have found your feet and the business begins to pay its way, you might come to resent the restrictions imposed upon you. That, however, is the deal. You forego the freebooting independence of a go-it-alone business person (almost certainly not something you wanted in the first place) for the surer, safer prospect of having a guiding hand at your elbow. You should, however, be aware at the outset of exactly what you are letting yourself in for, in terms of both the constraints that will be imposed on you and the continuing outflow of funds that will be required from you. Nothing is for nothing, and the franchisor will almost certainly want a regular share of your sales income in return for everything he has done for you.

If all this sounds unduly downbeat, it is not meant to be. But the purpose of a book such as this is not to present an uncritical endorsement, still less an advertisement. What is at stake is too important for that. Buying a franchise is not like buying a new kitchen or even a new house. It is an investment in a whole new way of life. Failure is not lightly shrugged off, it can really hurt. That is why a prospective franchisee should liken himself or herself to a general preparing for a campaign. To maximise the prospect of a successful outcome, you must be fully equipped, well briefed and properly armed. The aim of this book is to send you into the field with everything you need to secure a satisfactory result. And if that suggests that there are people out to get you, I am afraid there are. The world of franchising is not without its rogues and villains. Fortunately, they can easily be avoided if you know what to look for.

It would be wrong to end this introduction on a pessimistic note. As the following pages illustrate in detail, franchising has many success stories to tell, some of them spectacular. It would not be such an enduring feature of the economy if that were not the case. And for those who want a measure of independence, a comfortable income, and a better alternative to working for a faceless organisation that offers no clear link between the effort you put in and the rewards you take out, franchising is an answer made, if not in heaven, in a less imperfect corner of our world than most.

I hope that in this book you will find the inspiration to join the many thousands of people all over the world who are enjoying fulfilling lives as franchisees, and the determination to make the right choice for you.

1
For yourself, but not by yourself

The appeal of franchising

When you wake up in the morning do you look forward to the beckoning day? Does the prospect of another stint in the office, or at the factory, or behind the wheel, set your pulse racing? Do the hours fly past in a whirl of contented and rewarding endeavour? Is it with a sense of fulfilment that, at last, you head for home, cheek by jowl with fellow commuters, not all smelling as sweetly as they might; or nose to tail with other drivers, not all as composed and genial as they might be? Do you thrill to the prospect of the same again tomorrow, and the day after, and the day after that? Always assuming, of course, that you do not fall victim to a sudden bout of downsizing. Do you, in short, feel that you are valued?

I thought not. Otherwise you wouldn't have bought this book, or at any rate picked it up and flicked through it. There is in each of us a yearning – felt more keenly by some than others – for self-employment, the power to control our own affairs, to shape our destiny, to cease being a cog and instead own the machine and, with it, the right to pull its gleaming levers. Wouldn't it be nice, we dream, to answer to no one but ourselves (oh, all right, ourselves and the taxman), to shape the day rather than have it shape us; above all, to reap the undiluted rewards of our efforts and not to see a good part of them absorbed in some greater entity beyond our control, namely the boss's wallet? Then again – and here the dream bursts like a soap bubble – starting up a business from scratch is a horribly risky thing to do, especially when all you have known is to work for others. Just think of the obstacles: raising finance, finding premises, employing staff, controlling cash flow (assuming it flows at all), dealing with the Inland Revenue, Customs & Excise and sundry other meddlesome bureaucrats, winning customers (a terrifying thought: supposing no one wants to buy your goods or services?), haggling with suppliers etc.

And then there's the little matter of coming up with a great business idea in the first place, something that you can offer that no one else is already offering, or, more feasibly, something you can offer better and cheaper than someone else. No, it's all too much. Better to stick with the wage slaving. It's not so bad, come to that. There's the social life in the office (those happy chats around the water cooler); the pay may not be that great, but it's regular; the boss may be a tyrant, but he has his nice side (you see it once a year at Christmas); and there is such a thing as a comfort zone. Why take a chance and go it alone? It's a jungle out there. Better the devil you know.

There is however – and you may have heard of it in a different context – a 'Third Way', a system that provides the security of being part of a bigger organisation while at the same time giving you ownership and control of your own business. Too good to be true? Not really. Thousands of people are already working for themselves, building successful businesses, but with the help and encouragement of experts who have been there before, know the pitfalls, and can offer a guiding hand when it's needed. It's called franchising, and it really works. It's not foolproof by any means, as we shall see. But it's a darn sight better than the alternative, which is to stride off into the unknown and on your own, armed with little more than wishful thinking. There is, of course, a second alternative (though grammarians will tell you there can never be more than one) and that is to carry on chatting by the water cooler; but if that really is your preference self-employment is not for you.

Success stories

Real life examples of successful franchising are not difficult to find. There are almost certainly a few near you now. You've probably met dozens without knowing it. The man who unblocked your drain; the retailer who sold you those nice shoes; the woman who runs the takeaway pizza; and the couple who look after the indoor plants at the health club: they're all franchisees. The chances are that they used to do something else but for one reason or another – redundancy, boredom, or, best of all, a burning desire to do their own thing – they chucked it all in and bought a franchise. Here are some examples:

- Five years ago, husband-and-wife team Rob and Carol Shields opened the first UK branch of O'Briens Irish Sandwich Bar in Cambridge. They went on to open two more outlets, launch a large outside catering business, and develop new items that are now on O'Briens' menus around the world. Rob, a former construction industry manager, says, 'We took the humble sandwich and adapted it to suit people from all walks of life.'
- Trudy Hindmarsh runs a string of Stagecoach Theatre Arts outlets in Teesside, and counts among her achievements spotting the talent of Oscar-nominated *Billy Elliot* star Jamie Bell. She left her job as a senior teacher of a large primary school because she wanted to give children the chance to develop personally through drama and dance.
- In partnership with her husband Stuart, another former teacher, Jill Simpson, runs Rainbow International's cleaning franchise in Leicester. The couple built a turnover of more than £500,000 in less than four years and are consistently among the top five franchises in the network.
- Former welder Robert Tansley overcame the shock of redundancy to become a successful businessman running his own Chem-Dry carpet cleaning franchise in Nottingham. In 1993, he went into business with his 17-year-old son Christopher who, at the height of the recession of the early 1990s, was finding it difficult to get a job. Within a month Robert scored a personal triumph by winning the contract to clean all the carpets at his old workplace, Radcliffe Power Station, a contract he retains to this day. His turnover is approaching £1 million.
- Charles Williams quit farming in Cheshire 12 years ago because he saw no future in agriculture for him and his fiancée. Instead, he

took to the road in a mobile showroom and started selling cleaning products through Chemical Express International. Today the business is a highly profitable family affair.
- Former electrician Chris Barton combined drinks retailing with a post office and created a business generating some £90,000 a week. He already ran a successful off-licence in Congleton, Cheshire, when the opportunity came up to add a Post Office Counters franchise. The move increased his staff to 25, and his customer visits and turnover shot up by 25 per cent.

All of the above were either winners or finalists in the annual Franchisee of the Year competitions organised by the British Franchise Association, so it is fair to say that they are exceptional. But not all that exceptional. There are many hundreds of other successful franchisees across the country whose achievements, though unsung, are just as impressive as those who go in for awards. It would, however, be less than honest not to mention here that there are also franchisees who for one reason or another are disappointed, disenchanted or plain struggling. Franchising is not – as we shall have cause to warn throughout this book – a foolproof, still less easy, way either to make a lot of money or to blithely surf the waves of self-employment. Things can, and do, go wrong. The aim must always be to minimise the risks and make the right choice at the outset, and I hope that by the time you finish this book you will be well equipped to do just that. In the meantime, in setting your goals it does no harm to seek inspiration in the success stories. They are shining examples of what can be achieved, and proof that franchising works.

Franchising defined

That said, we now come to the task that anyone writing a book of this kind must face, and that is to define one's terms. What exactly is franchising and how does it work?

At this stage it is customary to talk about distributorships, licences and agency agreements, all of which are in some way or another related to franchising. Or to delve back into history, not just the recent past when Wimpy, ServiceMaster, Dyno-Rod and Kentucky Fried Chicken were the four lonely pioneers of UK franchising, but way back to the origins of the tied house system in the licensing trade, or even to the days when local barons granted rights to hold fairs and operate ferries. But none of this has much relevance when all you want to do is find a business that works for you. After all, when you are buying a car you do not need to know the inside leg measurement of Gottlieb Daimler.

When we talk about franchising today what we mean is 'business format franchising', a bundle of rights and properties wrapped up in a package and sold by a franchisor to a franchisee. Put at its simplest, when you a buy a franchise you buy a clone, a precise replica of a tried and tested business system. It's up to you to inject the spark of life that will set it in motion and provide the energy to keep it going and growing.

The franchise package

Let's undo the ribbon, open the franchise package and see what's inside. It should contain the following:

- an entire business concept with no bits missing, all outlined and explained in an operating manual;
- trade marks, logos, patents, and standard designs for the layout of premises, livery of vans, colour and pattern of uniforms;
- accounting and financial systems;
- training and help to set up the business;
- continuing help and back-up once the business is operating;
- a detailed contract.

Ideally, it will also contain:

- the legal right to operate in an exclusive territory; and
- marketing, public relations and advertising support.

Franchise investment

In return for the package the franchisee pays an initial franchise fee and continuing management services fees, or royalties on sales, and quite possibly regular contributions to an advertising fund. Usually the franchisor will expect the franchisee to make a significant personal investment in the business, topped up by bank finance where necessary, for the obvious reason that a large personal stake in an enterprise concentrates the mind and stimulates the energy.

The franchisee owns the business (though the franchisor retains control over the way in which the products and services are marketed and sold) and is free to dispose of it, within certain limitations, such as giving the franchisor the first right of refusal and the right to vet prospective buyers to ensure they will make suitable franchisees.

So you can see that in the best of all possible worlds the business format franchise offers one of the least risky ways of going into business for yourself. Arguably the most important safeguard of all is that the system has been pilot-tested for at least two or three years and has been shown to work. Add to that comprehensive training in how to organise and run the business, and continuing back-up and advice whenever you need it, and you might be forgiven for thinking that you couldn't go wrong. Sadly, however, things are never quite as straightforward as that. By no means all franchises are thoroughly tested before being offered for sale; some are very new ventures, which may or may not succeed, launched by franchisors who cannot wait to get their hands on franchisees' money.

Of course, it may be argued that to get in on the ground floor of a new enterprise holds out the prospect of greater rewards than going into a longer-established business with less scope for growth; and so it might, but it's risky and the whole point of franchising is to cut risk. And when it comes to training, the reality may be a skimpy two-day course, usually described as 'intensive' and/or 'comprehensive' and justifying neither term. I mention these hazards as an early warning that the best of all possible worlds has been postponed yet again and therefore the contents of the franchise package should be carefully examined, held up to the light, and tapped – you never know, they could be hollow.

The growth and diversity of franchising

That bona fide franchising works, however, is beyond doubt. Even allowing for the phenomenon that surveys tend to show what the people commissioning them want to see, the key findings of the NatWest/British Franchise Association Franchise Survey 2004, which relates to franchising during 2003, make encouraging reading:

- The number of business format franchises was 695, an increase of 3 per cent on the previous year.
- The annual turnover from the UK business format franchise sector was £9.65 billion, a 2 per cent increase on 2002.
- The employment generated by franchising is at the core of its contribution to the economy as a whole. It is calculated that 333,000 people are directly employed in the franchising sector – an increase of 1 per cent on the previous 12 months.
- 95 per cent of franchisees report profitability, up from 91 per cent in 2002.
- 86 per cent of franchisees regard their relationship with the franchisor as either definitely or mainly satisfactory.
- The ability to self motivate (68 per cent) and experience of sales and marketing (24 per cent) are the most important characteristics that franchisors seek in potential franchisees.
- Experience is very important to franchisors when recruiting new franchisees. Nearly two thirds of franchisees were in salaried employment immediately before taking out their current franchise, 29 per cent were self-employed outside franchising and just 2 per cent were self-employed with another franchise. Of the new recruits coming into franchising for the first time, only 12 per cent had previously been unemployed or made redundant.
- Almost all franchisors no longer specify a particular gender (93 per cent) or age range (91 per cent) when looking for suitable candidates to run a franchise. Nevertheless, the survey shows that only 28 per cent of franchisees are under the age of 40, compared with over 50 per cent in 1992 and that less than a third of new franchisees are women.

- As for making their final franchise selection, 20 per cent of franchisees opt for a well-known brand; 18 per cent have an interest in the particular field of activity; 16 per cent look at affordability; 7 per cent opt for a BFA member; 7 per cent look at the success of existing franchises; 3 per cent consider growth potential and 3 per cent simply liked the representative that they met from the franchise.

Just as impressive as the size of the franchising industry is its range and diversity. Lists are boring, but they make a point, so here goes: as a franchisee you could be cutting grass, hiring out hats, repairing furniture, doing a milk round, fitting kitchens, recruiting executives, training secretaries, touching up car paintwork, running slimming and dance classes, running a pub, managing a parcels service, managing property, advising on tax, refurbishing flat roofs, washing cars, distributing greetings cards, looking after elderly people, putting up estate agents' 'For Sale' boards, thatching roofs, freshening up wheelie bins, replacing locks, fixing hydraulic hoses, cutting hair, printing stationery, developing films, or cleaning carpets, or offices, or homes, or washrooms, or ovens, or computer equipment. As for selling, well, you could be selling fast food, pet food, chocolate, clothing, shoes, sports goods, hi-fi equipment, office products, fireplaces, second-hand goods, pine furniture. You could even be a private eye.

Yet for all the dazzling breadth of activities which it enfolds, franchising has its limitations. Not everything is franchiseable, and some things are more franchiseable than others. (A word of warning here: not everything that calls itself a franchise is a franchise. Part of the price of success that the industry has to pay is that it attracts fringe operators trying to pass off business opportunities as franchises. By no means all of these are disreputable; many can provide a source of income, but they are not franchises and should not be sold as such. Though business opportunity packages may have features in common with franchises, they tend to be more informal. They seldom involve detailed legally-binding contracts and agreements. There may be no royalties to pay but there may be little in the way of back-up either.)

Common features of franchises

Though franchise operations vary enormously in the kinds of goods or services they offer, the most viable, and therefore successful, have four features in common. In assessing a franchise you should satisfy yourself that all four are, as they say in the Army, present and correct.

Standardisation

We have already likened franchising to cloning, and the most remarkable feature of a clone is, of course, that it is identical in all obvious respects to every other taken from the same parent. So the first essential of franchise operation is that it can be **standardised**. The goods or services should be the same in every outlet; they should be offered for sale in the same way; and, no matter where the outlet, they should all be marketed in the same way, using the same brand name, logo, and image.

All this sameness may sound dull but it is essential for two reasons: it enables the franchisor to maintain a grip on the quality of the goods or service, whether they are sold in Plymouth or Pitlochry; and it gives customers the assurance that they will be getting the same reliable and predictable service from every outlet in the network.

USP

USP – a bit of jargon, this, borrowed from the world of advertising. It stands for **Unique Selling Proposition** and it's what makes a business stand out from the competition. Marketing people used fondly to imagine that every new product should have a USP, a magic comparable to that indefinable 'star quality' in a movie hopeful. However, experience slowly taught marketeers that uniqueness is a rare quality and usually the best you can hope for is something better than the competition such as, say, speed of service. But whether you call it a USP or something else, a franchise should have a property or quality that helps it stand out, and, better still, is hard to copy. An example might be a special process for removing dents from vehicle bodywork.

Ease of operation

Franchisees are drawn from all walks of life and bring to their new businesses a variety of skills and experience. In most cases they will be taking a complete change of direction – that's one of the attractions of franchising, it's a new start – bank managers metamorphose into indoor plants specialists, fighter pilots become publicans. But for franchising to work the new skills required of franchisees must not be too difficult to learn. As we have noted, the basic training is short – sometimes too short – and it is essential that what is taught is relatively easily understood, learnt, and put into practice. With practice and over time, the skills can be honed and built on, and experience is a great tutor. All the same, the key is **simplicity**.

High gross margin

Though experienced franchisees sometimes come to resent it, they owe their success not only to their own efforts but also to the franchisor, through whose ideas, systems, support and training their business was made possible. And, this being a cold commercial world, mere gratitude, even of the ungrudging variety, is not enough: the franchisor will usually want a continuing share in the franchisees' success in the shape of management services fees. It follows that each franchised outlet must be sufficiently profitable to provide an adequate return both to the franchisee and franchisor. And that in turn means that the **gross margin** on sales – the difference between the cost of providing the goods or service and the price paid by the customer – should be relatively high. A good everyday example is the takeaway, or home delivery, pizza, the basic ingredients of which account for only a fraction of the price paid by the customer.

Types of franchise

Before we move on to outline the arguments for and against buying a franchise – for it is a painful fact that in this imperfect world every pro has its con – it might be useful to describe the different categories of franchise, of which there are generally agreed to be four.

Job franchises

These usually involve supplying, selling and delivering products or services, often from a van. Typically a job franchise will involve a trade such as plumbing or car repairs. This kind of franchise is usually small, often taking the form of a one-man or woman business, though it is not uncommon for a partner (both in the sense of business partner and live-in partner) to share in the running of the business, perhaps taking orders and doing the paperwork while the operator is out on the road fixing drains or cleaning carpets.

The principal advantage of a job franchise is that it is normally a home-based business with small overheads. Job franchises are also at the cheaper end of the investment range. Although this kind of operation begins as a single person business, it need not stay that way: some franchisors encourage job franchisees to take on extra vans, employ staff, and make the transition to a management franchise.

Management franchises

These tend to be in business-to-business activities, such as secretarial training or staff recruitment, and based in office premises. The investment will be higher than for a job franchise and the business will almost certainly entail employing staff. The franchisor will normally expect potential franchisees to have previous managerial or organisational experience, though, as noted above, it is possible to acquire such skills within a franchise operation.

Retail franchises

Selling goods or services from a shop has always been a popular route into self-employment. The obvious snags, however, are difficulty in finding suitable premises, the expense involved in fitting them out, and the rising costs of retailing, especially in the high street. Franchising may overcome some of these problems. For example, the franchisor should be expert in locating premises, assessing their likely profitability, and fitting them out. Also, the franchisee may benefit from trading under an established brand name and in premises readily recognised by their logo, colour schemes, and so on. Even so, a retail franchise can be relatively expensive.

Investment franchises

The franchisee invests money in a franchise, for example a hotel, but delegates the management to someone else. The required investment is usually too large for any one franchisee, so he or she may be part of a syndicate. This kind of franchise is not really what this book is about. What concerns us is how private individuals can own and run a businesses through franchising.

Whatever kind of franchise you may choose, there are going to be advantages and disadvantages. And since franchising is a kind of partnership between you and the franchisor, it is only right and proper that the other party to the agreement also has to contend with disadvantages as well as advantages. The following is a summary of the upsides and downsides looked at from both points of view.

Advantages and disadvantages of franchises

Advantages for the franchisee

- **A proven business concept**, with a well-known trade name, corporate image, and tried and tested product or service. This should make it much easier to get started than would be the case for someone going it alone from scratch.
- **Reduced risk**. Any new business venture involves the possibility of failure or a disappointment, but franchising, while not completely eliminating risk, sets out to contain it. It does this through pilot testing,

training franchisees, and offering them continuing support and encouragement.
- Franchisees should be able to buy supplies, ingredients, equipment and so on at **favourable rates** owing to the bulk purchasing power of the franchisor.
- **Easier finance**. The high-street banks, no pushover as far as business is concerned, have come to recognise franchising's advantages over other start-ups, and are usually prepared to make finance more readily available for new outlets of recognised franchises.
- **Previous experience not required**. Few people have run their own businesses before and many are unwilling to embark on what is often a lonely and arduous venture. Franchising's singular contribution to the economy is to take people with no previous experience of self-employment and equip them to start their own independent businesses. And because a franchisee is part of a larger, supportive organisation there is not the sense of isolation that can afflict business people who set off on their own.
- **Exclusive territory**. It is usual for the franchisor to grant to a franchisee exclusive rights within a geographical territory, often a postcode area. This offers a measure of protection against competition but only of course from others within your network; there is nothing to stop franchisees from another competing franchise from muscling in on your patch.
- As a franchisee you enjoy a sense of **independence** and, all being well, should see a direct relationship between the success of your business and the effort that you put into it.

Disadvantages for the franchisee

- **Limited freedom.** Although, as a franchisee, you are the legal owner of the business, you are not the sole master of its destiny. Your freedom of manoeuvre is curtailed and hedged around by the terms of your contractual agreement. Most importantly, the franchisor retains control, often down to small details, over the way the product or service is presented to the customer and, quite possibly, over day-to-day procedures in running the business. This may be acceptable in the early stages when you are finding your feet, but, as you become more proficient, you may come to resent centralised control and long for the freedom to add some creativity of your own. (To be fair, the degree of central control varies from franchise to franchise: some franchise companies encourage franchisees to come up with their own ideas. But, as a general rule, franchisors understandably place great importance on keeping a tight rein on quality and consistency.)

To be blunt, the best franchisees are those prepared to follow the systems laid down in the manuals and accept that much of their success is down to the franchisor.

- **Service charges**. Just as experienced franchisees may find central control and monitoring irksome, so too may they bridle at the continuing requirement to pay service charges, especially if, as might be the case with more mature franchise outlets, less use is made of the franchisor's services.
- **Lack of flexibility.** What with manuals and systems and formats, it is in the nature of a franchise to be fairly inflexible. This may not be a problem if the market itself remains unchanged. However, it is not in the nature of markets to stand still. New competition may come along, new technology may arrive, and local conditions may change. The inherent rigidity of the business format may make the franchisor flat-footed when what is needed is a nimble response.
- **Exposure to bad publicity**. You are judged by the company you keep, which is fine when the franchisor has a good reputation. But should something go wrong at head office, leading to bad publicity nationally, it might have a detrimental effect on your business, even though you may be miles away and completely blameless. Similarly, if another franchisee in the network attracts bad publicity it can have an effect throughout the organisation.
- **The franchise may not be all it was cracked up to be**. Forecast sales may not materialise; the franchisor may not fully meet his obligations; most disastrously of all, the whole business might go bust. Some franchises are mis-sold or oversold, which is why the potential

franchisee must be on his or her guard and should, before the agreement is signed, take professional advice. (See Chapter 7.)
- There will almost certainly be **restrictions on terminating the contract** and/or selling the business.

Advantages for the franchisor

- **Rapid expansion.** The franchisor is able to expand his business using other people's money. Franchisees provide the capital to open new outlets, enabling the franchisor to build a chain more rapidly than might be possible through relying on his own resources alone, or borrowing money, or raising equity finance. Rapid geographical coverage is especially advantageous when a new product is being brought to market; to be one step ahead of the competition is fine, to be a country mile in front is better still.
- **Better management performance.** Because franchisees own and run each new outlet, they are almost certainly better motivated, harder working, and keener to contain costs than are salaried managers. This wellspring of dedicated energy helps the franchisor to increase market share, maximise efficiency and improve profitability.
- Franchisees are recruited locally and bring to the business **the benefits of local knowledge** and possibly contacts.
- In some respects, the franchisor has **greater control** over each outlet than might otherwise be possible with a geographically widespread chain. This is because to some extent franchisees are tied to the franchisor: they may, for instance, be obliged to buy supplies or equipment from the franchisor. Each outlet in the network sells the franchisor's products or services and no others, which is preferable to having them on sale alongside a competitor's products. The franchisor decides how the products are to be presented and sold, further enhancing his ability to maintain margins.
- Since each outlet is owned and run by the franchisees, they assume responsibility for tasks such as staffing, payroll, and controlling operating costs. This allows the franchisor to maintain a relatively **small head office staff.**

Disadvantages for the franchisor

- **Non-adherence to procedures**. We noted above that in some respects the franchisor has greater control. In others he doesn't. Although franchisees are not wholly independent business people, they nevertheless enjoy sufficient independence not to be easily bossed about. This makes them a very different proposition from salaried staff who can be hired and fired and more easily kept in line. The greater the franchisee's streak of independence the less may be his willingness to stick to the laid down procedures and ways of doing business, upon which much of the franchise format rests.
- Franchised outlets tend to be **less profitable** than company-owned outlets, mainly because the franchisor has to share the gross profits with the franchisee.
- **The relationship with the franchisees may become fraught**, particularly where the franchisee begins to resent what he sees as the interference of the franchisor. Management services charges can be another source of friction. Even where there is not open friction, a resentful franchisee may withhold information that may be of use to the franchisor. In a healthy franchise relationship there should be team spirit, trust, and a free exchange of information between franchisee and franchisor.
- **Underperformance**. Should the franchisor be unfortunate enough to recruit an inadequate or lazy franchisee who nevertheless operates within the terms of the franchise contract, there is not much that he can do about it. In extreme cases the franchisor may be obliged to offer to buy back an outlet from an unsatisfactory franchisee, perhaps at an inflated price.
- There is always the chance that a franchisee, having learnt about the business from the inside, may leave and set up **a rival operation**. Because of that risk, many franchise contracts stipulate that a departing franchisee must not operate a similar business within a specified time of leaving the organisation.
- **Trust**. The franchisor cannot be certain that the franchisee is making a full and honest declaration of his business activity. This can lead to difficulties in recovering sufficient fees from franchisees.

- **Investment.** Although a franchisor is able to grow his business rapidly using other people's money, it does not follow that launching a franchise requires little capital. A franchisor who goes properly about his business will need to invest a considerable sum in pilot testing, developing the package, and recruiting and training franchisees. He will incur all these costs before receiving any income from franchise fees or royalties. Moreover, until the franchise network builds up its sales the franchisor can expect modest returns, and will therefore need sufficient working capital to keep going until he reaches break-even point.

Successful franchise relationships

In summary then, franchising's great strength is that it is a way of starting and running a business with fewer of the risks that lie in wait in other types of new venture. But when you come to look at the pros and cons of franchising, both from the point of view of franchisors and franchisees, it becomes plain that the whole field is strewn with risk. Much of that, however, comes down to the relationship between the franchisor and the franchisee. In many ways it is a curious relationship: the franchisor owns the rights to the franchise format, but the franchisees own the outlets; the franchisor has control over some aspects of the business but not others. Additionally, in most businesses control derives from ownership, but in franchising control comes from selecting the right people in the first place and adopting a management style which rests more on encouragement and persuasion than on handing down orders.

For a franchised network to thrive and flourish there must be a reasonably harmonious relationship between the two parties to the agreement. It is rather like a marriage. There must be mutual trust if it is to last, and the whole success or failure of the undertaking depends on making the right choice of partner at the outset. Matching the right franchisee to the right franchisor is the single most important element in all of franchising. It is no use having a brilliant business concept, a scrupulously pilot-tested operation, a meticulously detailed franchise agreement, and an ingenious marketing plan if you then recruit franchisees who, for one reason or another, have not got what it takes. Similarly, it is no use having bags of energy and ambition, a burning desire to be self-employed, and the necessary capital tucked away to invest in a franchise if you then go out and choose a business that, for one reason or another, turns out to be a lemon.

The following chapters set out to help you avoid marrying a lemon.

2
Know yourself as others know you

From what you have read so far, does franchising appeal to you? Does it really?

I ask the question twice not because there is any reason to doubt the sincerity of your first reply, but to prepare you for what's coming. You might as well get used to having questions fired at you from the outset because this chapter is about little else.

Personal strengths and weaknesses

It's a truism of franchising that not everyone is cut out for self-employment. Though many people may dream of being their own bosses, for most of them it remains just that, a dream. They may attend franchise exhibitions and buy franchise magazines but for them it never goes any further. It's a way of living a little of the dream without allowing too much reality to intrude and burst the illusion. These people know in their hearts they are not cut out for self-employment. Though franchisors may find them a nuisance – 'time wasters' is the dismissive label attached to people who are not serious prospects – they involve far less work than those who sincerely believe they have what it takes, but, in truth, do not. Of those there are plenty, to judge from the conversion ratio, ie the percentage of applicants who are chosen as franchisees: no one knows the precise figure but it is certainly fewer than five per cent and may be no more than two per cent.

There are countless reasons why so many are turned down, but if you were to seek a single explanation it is that franchisees are a special kind of people who turn out to be quite rare. As we have seen, they need the gritty ambition of an entrepreneur but the docility, if not of a mouse, at least of a fairly biddable hound.

They are, in the words of a US franchising expert, Michael H. Seid, 'entrepreneurs lite'. They are presented with a ready-made system and it is their task to follow it, not to impose their own personalities and preferences on it. An entrepreneur lite, says Seid, takes the basic system and makes it better – not by changing the menu, but by providing, say, cleaner washrooms or by training staff to provide exceptional customer service. 'A great franchisee improves the performance of the system simply through better execution.'

From this follows the first set of questions that a prospective franchisee should ask himself or herself:

- **Do you always know better?** Can you accept the systems laid down? Can you swallow your pride and get on with it even though you think there may be a better way?
- **Do you itch to do things your way?** Are you forever thinking of alternatives to existing systems? If the franchisor says a shop should be laid out one way, would you prefer another?
- **Do you fancy yourself as something of a marketing expert?** Will you be content to accept that the franchisor's advertising and promotional material will work for you, or do you think you can come up with something better?
- **Are you loath to subordinate your wishes to those of the team?** Franchises are networks that require everyone to pull together in the same direction and to allow themselves to be absorbed into a standardised whole. Is this for you?
- **Do you like to keep your cards close to your chest?** The franchisor will want you to divulge details of your business, including financial information. From time to time people from head office may visit your outlet, ask questions and want to look at records, including

perhaps your tax returns. Will you be prepared to accept these intruders with good grace and listen to their advice?

If the honest answer to these questions is 'yes' then it ought to come as no surprise to learn that you are not made for franchising. You have about you much more of the full-bodied, premium-strength entrepreneur than the entrepreneur lite sought by franchisors.[1]

Every guide to franchising that was ever written – and this one is no exception – urges prospective franchisees honestly to assess their own strengths and weaknesses, often as a very first step to be taken long before beginning in earnest the search for a suitable business. It is, however, one of those glib instructions: rather like a golf professional's advice 'just swing through the ball', it's easily said, less easily done. How do you honestly assess your own strengths? Where do you begin? Do you think to yourself, 'Well, I'm not bad at getting up in the morning. And I don't mind hard work, as long as it's well paid. And, er, well, that's about it.' As for weaknesses, do you admit to the odd streak of impatience perhaps, or a willingness on occasions to cut corners? Do you confess – only to yourself, mind – to the greater sin of not much fancying the idea of selling, or at any rate cold calling?

And what's this thing called commitment? It's a word that trips off the tongue of every franchisor who is looking for likely franchisees. 'Suitable candidates will be hard-working, ambitious, good at people skills and have commitment.' 'We are looking for committed people.' (Not to be confused with people who have been committed.) It means, I think, that franchisors want franchisees who will be dedicated to the business rather than half-hearted. But then they would, wouldn't they? It's rather like the manager of a Formula 1 racing team saying that he wants drivers who go

---

[1] Interestingly, research on both sides of the Atlantic shows that around half of all franchisees have previous experience of self-employment, either through working for themselves or as a result of being brought up in a family whose parents were self-employed. This reinforces the notion that the entrepreneurial spirit lives on in franchisees, albeit in a diluted form, which allows them to trade off complete independence in exchange for the safety net of the franchisor's knowledge and systems.

fast. Few people are going to admit to being half-hearted or potential quitters, either to themselves or to a franchisor.

How do you reconcile the need to present yourself in the most favourable light possible, and to believe in yourself, with the need privately to admit to failings? And do those failings matter? After all, no one is perfect, and you can't tell me that all those hundreds of successful franchisees out there are paragons, achievers without blemish.

Your self-assessment

Plainly all the questions that would-be franchisees must ask themselves have to be ordered, categorised, tabulated and valuated. And the results must be capable of being totted up, assessed and formed into a conclusion – have you got what it takes or haven't you? In other words, what's needed is a questionnaire, of which there are many. Most, however, content themselves merely with putting the questions: 'Do you think you have the skill to market and sell?' 'Would you be any good at motivating staff?' The honest answer may be that you think so, but can't be sure. Unfortunately, unlike an opinion poll, which allows you to be a don't-know, a self-assessment questionnaire should probe deeply and reach the answers despite your diffidence or uncertainty. It's a tall order, but Professor John Stanworth of the University of Westminster, and an expert in franchising, has risen to the challenge.

He has devised a 'diagnostic questionnaire' which operates on a 'forced choice' principle. Each question offers a choice of three responses: (a), (b), and (c). Prospective franchisees are asked (or ask themselves) to select the statement under each question that most accurately describes them. They should choose one of the responses to the exclusion of the others. There can be no sitting on the fence.

The questionnaire

Question 1 Are you regarded by those who know you as:
(a) Generally a fairly self-contained person? (2)
(b) Generally a rather gregarious person? (0)
(c) Somewhere in between (a) and (b)? (1)

Question 2 Are you regarded by those who know you as:
(a) Frequently frustrated by tasks you find boring? (0)
(b) Able to endure a reasonable amount of boredom and frustration? (1)
(c) Generally good at concentrating on whatever tasks face you? (2)

Question 3 Would you say that:
(a) You possess an excess of mental and physical stamina and enjoy excellent health? (2)
(b) You find that you tire easily if you try to work long hours and your health is not always of the best? (0)
(c) You estimate that your health and stamina are about average for a person of your age? (1)

Question 4 Would you say that:
(a) You find mistakes and setbacks very demoralising? (0)
(c) You feel that mistakes can be a very useful way of learning as long as they are not repeated? (2)
(c) You try to learn from your mistakes but often find it easier said than done? (1)

Question 5 Which of the following most accurately describes you:
(a) You set yourself targets and almost obsessively chase after them? (2)
(b) You get fed up if you find yourself 'on the go' all the time? (1)
(c) You like to take life at a modest pace and respond to pressures as and when they arise? (0)

Question 6 Would you say that:
(a) You find it almost impossible to make tough decisions, particularly if they involve people? (0)
(b) You can make tough decisions when necessary but the process takes a lot out of you emotionally? (1)
(c) You see tough decisions as a fact of life – you don't necessarily enjoy them but, on occasions, see no alternative? (2)

Question 7 Would you say that:
(a) You do not suffer fools gladly and make little attempt to hide your feelings? (0)
(b) You have notable patience and self-control? (2)
(c) You are situated in between positions (a) and (b)? (1)

Question 8 Would you say that:
(a) Your mood is very influenced by events? (0)
(b) Your mood is very little influenced by events? (1)
(c) You tend to adopt a policy of 'taking the rough with the smooth'? (2)

Question 9 Are you regarded by people who know you as:
(a) A person who needs to know exactly where they stand? (0)
(b) A person who can live with uncertainty? (2)
(c) A person who can endure a reasonable amount of uncertainty? (1)

Question 10 If you go into business would you:
(a) Resent people who appear to be trying to tell you how to run your own business? (0)
(b) Regard the views of others as a potential source of useful information and guidance? (2)
(c) Be willing to listen to others when you had the time but likely to 'take it all with a pinch of salt'? (1)

Question 11 Would you say that your total personal assets and savings together:
(a) Exceed the full buy-in cost of the franchise? (2)
(b) Exceed two-thirds of the full buy-in cost? (1)
(c) Amount to less than two-thirds of the full buy-in cost? (0)

Question 12 Do you feel that your spouse:
(a) Feels that how you earn your living is very much your own affair? (0)
(b) Would prefer to see you doing something you enjoyed? (1)
(c) Is very keen on your taking a franchise and willing to back you very strongly? (2)

Question 13 Which of the following is true of you:
(a) There is no history of self-employment in your family involving either yourself or close relatives? (0)
(b) Though you have not personally been self-employed previously, there is some history of self-employment in your family via close family and/or relatives? (1)
(c) You have personally been self-employed previously? (2)

Question 14 Is your main reason for wanting to be a franchisee:
(a) To achieve a good standard of living? (2)
(b) Because most of the alternative options for making a living appear closed? (1)
(c) For the independence and autonomy involved in having your own business? (0)

Question 15 Do you feel that, in taking a franchise:
(a) You would have a tried and tested product/service which should sell itself? (0)
(b) No matter how good the product/service, customers still respond to sales effort? (1)
(c) Selling would still be a key activity? (2)

Question 16 Is your prior work experience:
(a) Unrelated to the franchise in question? (2)
(b) Very closely related to the franchise in question? (0)
(c) Marginally related to the franchise in question? (1)

Question 17 In running your own business, would you:
(a) Prefer to stay small? (0)
(b) Wish to grow as much as circumstances allowed? (2)
(c) Grow to a size where you could begin to take more time out of the business? (1)

Question 18 Do you feel that:
(a) To get a job done properly, you must do it yourself? (0)
(b) Delegation allows you to spend your time doing what you are best at? (2)
(c) Delegation is a necessary evil? (1)

Question 19 Do you usually feel that it pays to:
(a) Take a long-term view of things? (2)
(b) Make hay while the sun shines? (0)
(c) Adopt a medium-term view? (1)

Question 20 Do you feel that:
(a) Your future lies largely in your own hands? (2)
(b) You can at least influence your own future? (1)
(c) The individual is merely a puppet on the end of a string and can do little to influence events? (0)

Analysing the results

There is nothing complicated or concealed about the marking: the higher your tally of points, the better your chances of succeeding as a franchisee. Professor Stanworth says that a good score would be in the 20–30 range.

It goes without saying that in any self-assessment there is no point in cheating, for you have only yourself to fool. The real value of the exercise is that it gives you an insight not only into your own capabilities – and makes you think about them in the process – but also into the abilities that franchisors are looking for.[2] Professor Stanworth sums them up as follows. Each question relates to a different desirable quality – the franchisee should be able to:

Q1 cope with the isolation of self-employment;
Q2 exercise self-discipline;
Q3 work long hours under pressure;
Q4 learn from failure;
Q5 compete with self-imposed standards;
Q6 take unpopular decisions;
Q7 resist impetuous or emotional behaviour;
Q8 take a balanced view of events;
Q9 tolerate uncertainty;
Q10 accept advice;
Q11 demonstrate financial viability;
Q12 demonstrate support of spouse;
Q13 demonstrate enterprise background;
Q14 demonstrate profit motivation;
Q15 demonstrate sales orientation;
Q16 demonstrate receptiveness towards franchisor's training;
Q17 demonstrate growth orientation;
Q18 demonstrate a favourable attitude towards task delegation;
Q19 take the long-term view;
Q20 demonstrate belief that individuals can 'make things happen'.

---

2 The questionnaire does not apply with unwavering rigour to all franchised businesses. Some franchisors, for instance, may not want franchisees who are hugely ambitious, preferring instead people who are content to limit their horizons to serving their territories well. And, although some franchisors may prefer recruits to have no previous experience in the business in question, others may see it as an advantage. Generally speaking, however, the 20 questions cover the ground well.

Here are the issues looked at in more detail:

Q1 Ability to cope with isolation – in contrast to being an employee, you have no boss, or other people in the same organisation doing the same job, who can give help, advice and moral support. To put it more precisely, it is usually of little concern to anyone else whether you succeed or fail.

Q2 Ability to exercise self-discipline – in running your own business, you're responsible for a wide range of tasks. Some of these you will almost certainly find satisfying whilst others will prove highly frustrating. There is no one but yourself responsible for allocating your time and you can, at your peril, neglect tasks such as paperwork, financial control, invoicing and chasing payment. Although all these tasks may appear to be stopping you from getting on with the 'real job' of producing and selling, no business can survive without them.

Q3 Ability to work long hours under pressure – in running your own business you are seldom off duty. Thus you require both mental and physical stamina. In the early days of a new business, there is little time for leisure activities, holidays or illness. Some advisers go as far as to recommend that anyone setting up a new business should consult their doctor first.

Q4 Ability to learn from failure – disappointments are inevitable in business and can lead to demoralisation. A good businessman, however, must possess the resilience to survive setbacks and learn from them.

Q5 Ability to compete with self-imposed standards – when working for yourself, targets and standards need to be set which act as goals reinforcing motivation. If these goals are set too low they have little motivating force. If they are set unrealistically high, they will not be achieved and a sense of failure and demoralisation may result. Thus, modestly ambitious, though not unrealistic, goals need to be set and used as markers of achievement.

Q6 Ability to take unpopular decisions – it is impossible to remain popular at all times and any attempt to do so is likely to have costly consequences for your business.

Q7 Ability to resist impetuous or emotional behaviour – in the face of frustration, it is tempting to react in what might later be seen as a whimsical manner that is not in the longer-term interests of the business. This may be emotionally satisfying in the short term but should be resisted at all costs – emotions must be kept under control.

Q8 Ability to take a balanced view of events – it is easy to yield to the temptation of feelings of euphoria or depression in response to good or bad news. This can prove extremely stressful and wearing. A successful businessman needs to be able, at all times, to take a balanced view of events, to 'take the rough with the smooth'.

Q9 Ability to tolerate uncertainty – in an environment dominated by large organisations, the setting up of a new business is a highly creative venture and requires a facility for surviving uncertainty. People with a low tolerance of uncertainty experience difficulties in coping with the resulting stress.

Q10 Ability to accept outside advice – having gone into business to gain a certain level of independence, it often requires a determined effort to be able to seek out and act on external advice but, again, this capacity needs to be exercised.

Q11 Ability to demonstrate financial viability – though the clearing banks tend to lend to would-be franchisees more readily than to would-be conventional small business start-ups, it needs to be remembered that all loans have to be repaid, with interest. A large financial repayment overhead in the early days of trading can impose additional pressures.

Q12 Ability to demonstrate support of spouse – most franchise outlets involve long hours of working and domestic disruption. In a large proportion of cases there is some advantage to the spouse actually working in the running and/or administration of the business. Thus, anything less than positive support can have very negative consequences.

Q13 Ability to demonstrate an enterprise background – despite the desire for self-employment being quite common, relatively few make the leap from aspiration to reality. Those who have previous direct experience of self-employment or, alternatively, have had a close relative self-employed (usually a father) appear to find the transition easier. Some evidence exists to suggest that they may also be more successful in terms of business growth.

Q14 Ability to demonstrate profit motivation – amongst small business people generally, the desire for growth is of a rather low order and profit motivation is of a lower order than other goals such as independence and autonomy. Most small businesses, in fact, never employ anyone other than the owner. In the case of a franchise, however, the pressures to push for growth of profits and size of business are usually quite strong.

Q15 Ability to demonstrate sales orientation – despite national advertising and the promotion of brand awareness by the franchisor, sales skills on the part of the franchisee can still make a very substantial difference to levels of market penetration. Local advertising, and good interpersonal skills and service at the customer interface, can be crucial.

Q16 Ability to demonstrate receptiveness towards the franchisor's training – franchisors tend towards the view that 'starting with a clean sheet' is the best basis for a training programme rather than competing with, or attempting to displace, previous training that a potential franchisee may have already had in the field concerned.

Q17 Ability to demonstrate growth orientation – the income of the franchisor is directly related to the growth of franchisees. Thus, franchisees easily satisfied with low levels of growth may require considerable motivating.

Q18 Ability to delegate – one serious growth constraint on most small businesses is the lack of willingness or ability to delegate.

Q19 Ability to take a long-term view – in an economy suffering from endemic 'short-termism', long-term planning and goal setting is likely to pay dividends.

Q20 Ability to make things happen – people with an 'internal locus of control' tend to believe that they personally can influence their environment. This belief can become a self-fulfilling philosophy.

From the above you get a good idea of the ingredients from which the perfect franchisee is made. Such a paragon, however, is a rare beast; very few people combine the saintly qualities of tolerance, self-discipline, willingness to learn, calmness of disposition, fortitude in the face of setbacks, courage in dealing with others, and a single-minded devotion to success. That said, there is no getting away from the need to be tough and hard working. And if you can accept with good grace that you are in partnership with a franchisor and it's thanks to him or her that you are running a business, so much the better.

Be honest with yourself: if the idea of eating, drinking and sleeping business day after day doesn't appeal to you, the chances are that you will be better off staying a wage earner. When you are employed by someone else there's always the boss or the management to blame when things go wrong, and, with luck, you can put all the bother and the hassle behind you when you step out of the factory or the office at the end of the day. As a franchisee you carry the can (you can always try blaming the franchisor, or your staff, or the weather, but much good will it do you) and you can't escape. Either you master your destiny or it will master you.

If all this sounds like the advice of a Dutch uncle (and a particularly irritating one at that) it's because one cannot over-emphasise the need for honest self-analysis. Far better to admit defeat at this stage than to put yourself through the rigours of searching for a suitable franchise, going through the selection process and, assuming you succeed in bluffing your way in, discovering that you simply cannot hack it. It would all be such a dispiriting waste of time and money.

But – and here we put aside the hat of the Dutch uncle and don instead the rose-tinted glasses of the cheery optimist – if you scored 20 or 30 points in the questionnaire, if you are absolutely determined to be your own boss, albeit with the help of others, and if you have the wholehearted support of those near and dear to you, give it a go. Many others have, and many have succeeded.

3
When all is not what it seems

Question: when is a franchise not a franchise? Answer: when it's a business opportunity.

Depending upon your choice of metaphor, the search for the perfect franchise will take you across a minefield, over an obstacle course, or through a maze. Whichever route you follow you are bound to encounter difficulties. Chief among these are, does the business that interests you really suit you?, and is it all it appears to be? Later chapters will help you to check both of these, but before we even get that far there is a nuisance item that needs to be got out of the way. Everyone knows that the last resort of someone who is losing an argument is to ask his opponent to define his terms, which serves as both a delaying tactic and a red herring. But, much though I should like to avoid a wearisome discussion that involves defining terms, the craftiness of the marketplace forces us into telling the sheep from the goats, and that means defining them. Now, of course, no one can define a sheep or a goat, or an elephant for that matter – you know one when you see one. If only it were that easy with franchising and business opportunities, but it's not.

Franchise or business opportunity

In your search for a franchise you are bound to come across businesses that describe themselves as franchises but are in fact goats: they may look like a franchise, they may feel like a franchise and for all I know they might smell like a franchise, but they are something else – they are, in short, business opportunities. This straight away plunges us into a definitional problem: for although all franchises are by definition business opportunities, not all business opportunities are franchises. To make matters more confusing still, the boundaries between the two often overlap, so that a business opportunity may have some of the characteristics of a franchise: it might, for example, offer training and a measure of continuing support. Nor do I wish to imply that business opportunities are necessarily dodgy enterprises best avoided. Many are no doubt sound propositions that offer genuine prospects of a return on your investment. But you must be clear about the nature of the operation into which you are being invited to pump your cash: a franchise is attractive primarily because it is a tried and tested business system and therefore less risky than starting a small business from scratch. A business opportunity seldom meets those criteria in quite the same way or to quite the same degree. So, in the absence of a DNA kit, how on earth do you tell these animals apart?

The franchise

The most distinguishing feature of a franchise – in fact its very essence – is that it is a complete business package. A fully-formed, well established, franchise is a business system with a known brand that has been proven in the marketplace and has a number of trading franchisees who are enjoying some success. In return for a fee, the franchisee receives training, continuing support and guidance and, depending on the contract, advertising and promotional back-up. But that isn't all: as part of the deal the franchisee will sacrifice some independence (this is because the franchisor retains the right to make sure everyone in the network is, to borrow a cliché from the politicians, singing from the same song sheet) and will almost certainly be required to part with a percentage of his turnover in the shape of monthly royalties. In short, a franchise allows you to open for business as the independent outlet (with one or two strings attached) of an established enterprise with a good name and a proven reputation.

The business opportunity

A business opportunity differs from a franchise in two key respects. First, in a business opportunity you pay for the system, the products and perhaps the training and, thus equipped, you can go off and start a business. Generally speaking, that is the end of your relationship with the vendor, unless the deal requires that you continue to buy stock from him. He is unlikely to offer continuing training, support and advice, and will have no obligations to do so. Second, a business opportunity is unlikely to require you to stick to strict guidelines and follow the laid-down systems; you can go off and do your own thing.

So what types of activities are sold as business opportunities? Two of the most common are distributorships and what the Americans call 'rack jobbers'. As a distributor you have the right to sell products supplied by the business opportunity and make a profit on the sale. You may be given some coaching in product knowledge and sales techniques but you will be on your own, answering to yourself and relying on your ability to find and convert sales leads, though you may get some referrals from head office. A promising distributorship would be one that deals in a product with a unique selling point (for example a gadget that prevented car tyres from puncturing) that is not sold through normal retail outlets.

Rack jobbing involves setting up vending machines or point-of-sale display racks and regularly stocking them with merchandise supplied by the business opportunity. Typical items sold in this way are greetings cards, confectionery and CDs, and typical outlets are petrol station shops, garden centres, and small independent retailers such as grocers and newsagents. Retailers are often offered the merchandise on a no-sale-no-payment basis, which of course is a sound inducement to persuade them to cooperate. Typically, the person running the business opportunity will build up a 'round' of outlets – he or she may be supplied with an initial number by the business opportunity company to get things started – and will visit each on a regular, perhaps weekly, basis, to collect money and restock the racks. The proceeds are shared with the retailers. Another example of rack jobbing is the siting of vending machines in places of work such as shops, offices and factories, and restocking them with repeat purchase items such as sandwiches and snack foods. In almost all business opportunities of this type the operator undertakes to buy supplies from the company that sold him the opportunity, though in some cases he may be allowed to buy stock from other suppliers as well.

At this point it ought to be noted that rack jobbing is a good example of the way in which business opportunities and franchising shade into each other at the margins. For the British Franchise Association numbers among its members greetings card companies whose franchisees go about their business in much the way described above. What qualifies them as bona fide franchises is that they operate under a recognised brand, have formalised contractual agreements with their franchisees that last for a specified period, say five years, and have the benefit of continuing back-up from the parent company. Even so, there are grey areas here: for example, there are some franchising experts who doubt that franchised door-to-door milk rounds can truly be described as franchises, or feel that at any rate they are not in what might be called the first division.

While this book is designed primarily with the potential franchisee in mind, we cannot let this chapter pass without first outlining the relative benefits of franchising and business opportunities, and giving a brief summary of the way to choose a business opportunity.

Choosing a business opportunity

On the plus side, business opportunities have a number of advantages compared with franchising. First among these is that they offer far more independence and flexibility. Second, they can usually be run from home, as either a part-time or full-time business. Third, they tend to cost a lot less than a franchise. Finally, there are no royalty payments deducted from your sales revenue.

The main disadvantages are that business opportunities seldom include help in either setting up the business or running it. Nor, compared with franchising, is there likely to be much in the way of marketing back-up, training or continuing support. The absence of royalties is a coin with a reverse side: okay, you don't have to part with a percentage of turnover, but that also means that the company or individual who sold you the business opportunity has no vested interest in your continuing success.

And now for a big warning: if you are thinking of buying a business opportunity take care. There are bona fide opportunities, but there are also dodgy operations and some downright scams. Many a con artist has done well by placing small ads promising easy, quick returns from vending machines, work-from-home opportunities and the like, all in return for a small down payment. Of course, hundreds of small down payments from the gullible and the gulled all add up, and by the time the shyster is rumbled all you can see of him is the outline of a running figure with bulging pockets silhouetted on the horizon.

With that risk in mind, it obviously pays to investigate a business opportunity before parting with any money. The procedure I am about to outline may strike you as irksome, particularly if the outlay to acquire a business opportunity is relatively small. But think of it this way: you are tempted to invest (even if the amount is small) because you want some extra income and have been led to believe that the business in question has something to offer; how would you feel if it turns out to be a duff proposition? The answer may be summed up in a single word – cheated. And when you are cheated it doesn't matter how much money you invested, the grievance is still the same. So my advice is to investigate a business opportunity with diligence and never take the vendor's word as your sole assurance.

Here, then, is a checklist of the things to do before buying a business opportunity. The more of these tips you follow, the less likely you are to be taken for a ride:

- Try to find out how long the company has been in business. The longer established it is, the more reliable it is likely to be. You will pay more for an established concept than a newer one, but the risk is less.
- Make an assessment of the credibility of the company. Do you get the impression that what most interests it is taking your money? If so, keep your hand in your pocket.

- Find out how many other people are running the business opportunity. Ask the vendor if you can contact them and find out how satisfied they are. If this is not allowed, feel free to draw your own conclusions.
- Ask if there is anything in the way of training and support.
- Evaluate the product and try to satisfy yourself that there is a reasonable demand for it in your area.
- Make an estimate of the hours you will have to work in order to make the kind of money that will make the effort worthwhile.
- Stand back for a moment and ask yourself if you are cut out for this opportunity. In particular, will you feel confident in selling what is perhaps a new product or unusual service that potential buyers know nothing about?
- If the product or service in question is new or different, what is the business opportunity vendor offering in the way of sales aids and product knowledge? If there is a standard operating manual, that is a plus point.
- Ask for details of your costs and obligations. Will you be required to buy stock? If so, how much and at what price? Many an unwitting business opportunity buyer has found himself with a garage full of unsaleable wonder products that were going to make his fortune. Some of the best business opportunities – and franchises too for that matter – do not involve carrying stock at all; rather they work on the basis that you first make the sale and only then deliver the goods.

To sum up, not all business opportunities are to be avoided. Some may even be turnkey businesses providing everything you need to set yourself up. They may offer support, training, marketing, and some ready-made customers to get you started. The more of these features they have, the better. But unlike business format franchises, they are seldom branded outlets of the parent operation. The company's logo, name and the way in which it is run are usually decided solely by the individual operator. The final choice will be determined by your preference for safety versus freedom. The more you are risk-averse, the greater you will find the appeal of franchising.

4
The great franchise myth

The myth

Franchising in common with many industries has its own urban myths, that is, items of folklore of mysterious origin and doubtful authenticity, and I think it is only fair to warn you of one in particular that you are liable to hear uttered repeatedly, particularly by people trying to sell you a franchise.

It is this: whereas 95 per cent of franchises succeed, some 80 per cent of independent business start-ups fail.

You can see at a glance why it is such an enduring slogan. Its appeal is immediate; its selling power enormous. But it is a myth all the same, and one which you should discount without a second thought. That is not to say that the franchisor is deliberately lying when he repeats the mantra; he almost certainly believes it to be true. That is one of the reasons why it endures; it has become an unquestioned article of faith.

It's a fiction worth pursuing and examining in more detail because it leads to a greater understanding of why franchises might fail, and confirms what you will discover in this book about the ways to minimise risk in choosing a franchise. Fortunately, unlike some urban myths, this one can be traced to a source – the US Department of Commerce, no less. In the early 1980s the department compiled statistics on franchise failure in a series of reports called *Franchising in the Economy*. Though these have since been discontinued, everyone with a convenient memory recalls the claim that '95 per cent of all franchises are still in business after five years'. Indeed, it has been handed down like a folkloric item and has assumed an unquestioned veracity that seems immune to debunking.

The debunking

And that despite the fact that it has been debunked several times over. For instance James Cross, of the University of Nevada, says that although the Department of Commerce's attempts to compile statistics on franchise failures were commendable, they were based on 'potentially incomplete and inaccurate data submitted by franchisors'.

He and other debunkers say the statistics are misleading because many franchisee failures are disguised by changes in the ownership of the franchise outlet in question. In other words, a franchisee may go under, but because his business is then sold to someone else, who may or may not make a go of it, the disappointment and loss suffered by the first franchisee does not appear in the statistics. No one, however, least of all the unfortunate loser, could class the experience as anything other than a failure. As Cross says:

> Advocates of franchising often point to low failure rates as an advantage of this method of doing business, and low failure rates are widely quoted in various publications and franchisors' promotional materials. This is fine as long as readers are aware of what the failure rate actually measures. The turnover rate – closures plus transfers – may be a more meaningful statistic, since it measures the overall likelihood of actually remaining in business.

Another good reason to question the urban myth is that the surveys on which it is based ignore – or have concealed from them – the fly-by-night, unscrupulous operators masquerading as legitimate franchisors. This is more than simply a question of terminology. If you have been sold a franchise and it subsequently flops, it doesn't matter to you that it ought not to have been called a franchise in the first place. Once again, please take note of the tips in this book to make sure you are not sold a lemon disguised as a peach.

More doubt on the myth is cast by the fact that it is a weakness of surveys that the respondents tend to be self-selecting, with only the best and the most confident agreeing to answer the questions. After all, if you are a franchisor with an abnormally high failure rate, you are unlikely to boast about it in a questionnaire.

It's one thing to debunk a myth, quite another to put a bomb under it, which is what Timothy Bates, then a professor at Wayne State University in Detroit, achieved in the early 1990s. For his research suggested that not only do franchised businesses fail in larger numbers than the mythology maintains, their record is even worse than the ordinary business start-ups beside which they are supposed to look so good. After studying figures from the US Census Bureau Business Owners' Database, he concluded that 34.9 per cent of franchise businesses failed compared with 28 per cent of non-franchise businesses. He suggested that the difference in performance was due in part to franchises being over-represented in high-risk retailing and under-represented in services. He also suggested that other reasons for franchise failures included the recruitment of inadequate franchisees and the high level of franchisor fees and royalties.

Although the research is American, the principles underlying it and the conclusions drawn from it may be assumed to apply with equal validity in this country. Professor John Stanworth, of Westminster University, certainly thinks so. He says:

> It should be remembered that, while a franchisee should, and hopefully will, receive the kind of professional managerial help and advice which is not normally available to small and medium-sized enterprises, this is only delivered at a price and often a substantial one at that – typically an ongoing rate of around 10 per cent levied on a sales volume (in addition to front-end start-up fees and charges). Very many small companies would almost certainly not make total profits of this magnitude and, by any measure, this kind of royalty regime is likely to take in the region of half the total profits of even a well-run franchised outlet. In short, the royalty regime is a heavy burden for outlets to bear.

He adds that in so far as franchised businesses have a superior propensity for survival, that must in part be explained by the higher initial investment required than for normal start-ups. This is borne out by another

American study, which showed that initial investment is the best single predictive measure of success, and that franchise outlets typically have a rate of investment almost eight times as high as independents.

Professor Stanworth is himself an able debunker. In 1994, he decided to assess the survival level of a sample of 74 franchises known to be in existence 10 years earlier. The sample was judged to have represented between one-third and one-half of all the systems in existence in Britain at that time, and included many of the better-known systems. For instance, the list contained five of the original eight founder members of the British Franchise Association. It also contained a fairly strong representation of young franchises. The assessment of these companies was undertaken by a number of leading authorities drawn from the industry, for example franchise bankers, consultants and specialist journalists.

'The inescapable conclusion to emerge from this exercise is one of a high franchise attrition rate,' concluded Professor Stanworth. 'At best, one franchise company in four could be described as an unqualified success story over a ten-year period. Around half the sample was judged to have failed completely and utterly.

'Overwhelming evidence now suggests that only in the region of one quarter to one third of new franchise start-ups survive through to their tenth anniversary and it appears quite possible that only 50 per cent survive to their fourth anniversary.'

Again, although the research is by no means new, there is no reason to assume that the underlying circumstances are any different now from what they were then. This makes some pretty grim reading. However, the merit in dispelling fairy tales – and the franchising myth comes into that category – is that with the pixie dust swept out of the way the picture becomes much clearer, and in truth it is not as bleak as it might seem. Yes, franchises can, and do, fail. But when they do it is almost always because the rules have not been followed. Franchising is not a soft option, for either the franchisor or the franchisee. And yet both parties may be deluded by the optimism the industry generates on behalf of itself. Companies may be led to believe that franchising is a relatively easy and less costly way of expanding. Individuals may be led to believe that franchising is a fail-safe way of being a success. Neither assertion stands up to scrutiny.

As Professor Stanworth points out, it is true that when a company franchises its operation the cost of expansion is reduced because the franchisees bear much of the burden. But that saving can easily be offset by the high costs of pilot-testing and the even more expensive task of franchise system development through to break-even point. 'For a small business intent on developing into a credible franchise operation, the strains normally associated with small business growth are, in fact, likely to be magnified and concentrated rather than reduced.'

As for the prospective franchisee, his or her success will depend upon the care and diligence with which the selection process is carried out. Yes, you can make a success of franchising – many, many people have – but it would be crazy and irresponsible for me to suggest that franchising could ever be an easy option. The whole of this book is devoted to helping you go through the painstaking task of picking a franchise that will minimise the risk of failure and give you the best chance of finding a rewarding and fulfilling future.

The underlying truths

The franchise failure statistics, though far more alarming than the smokescreen of bullish advertising would have you believe, do little more than point up the underlying truths that are there to see if only you look more closely. In summary, they are as follows:

- To stand a chance of success, a franchise needs to be adequately funded, pilot-tested, and capable of generating sufficient returns to provide an adequate income for the franchisees, repay bank loans and loan capital, and meet the franchisor's demand for royalty fees of up to 10 per cent on sales turnover.
- Every franchise should have an operating manual to guide franchisees; a franchise contract setting out the legal obligations of both parties; and a franchised prospectus for recruiting franchisees.

- When franchising is aggressively promoted as a relatively easy way to go into business, in so far as the statement carries any credence at all it is as a description of franchising in general rather than of a particular franchise opportunity. Newer, and therefore riskier, franchises, trade on the mythological risk figure, and they make up the bulk of the more heavily promoted opportunities. So the more you are reminded that franchising is safe, the warier you should be.
- Potential franchisees must distinguish between marketing hyperbole and hard reality. Then they must work hard to ensure as far as possible that their chosen franchise is a business that suits their skills and abilities and has a good chance of meeting their aspirations.

5
The search begins

Narrowing the choice

As we have seen, the world of franchising is an ever-changing ferment of activity. There are almost 700 different franchises to choose from, operating across a wide range of business activities. You cannot possibly investigate them all, nor would you want to.

Start by looking at the broad sectors, of which there are six (there may be more, but six are enough to be getting on with). They are (with examples in brackets): hotels and catering (pubs, fast food outlets); retailing (clothes shops, second-hand goods); personal services (hairdressing, fitness clubs); property services (office cleaning, plumbing); transport and vehicle services (car valeting, vehicle repairs); and business and communication services (employment and training, print and design). It's obvious that these sectors require different aptitudes and it will be equally obvious to you whether or not you have (a) an interest in the field in question and (b) the personal qualities to make a go of it.

Playing to your strengths

We know from the last chapter that you do not necessarily need previous experience in the sector that appeals to you (indeed, some franchisors would far rather you came to them unburdened with knowledge of their industry). One of the great strengths of franchising is that it can take people from a wide variety of backgrounds and train them to run a business. That said, though franchising works, it cannot achieve miracles, nor can it defy commonsense. So if you are the kind of person who cannot pick up a hammer without hitting your thumb, it stands to reason you would be ill-suited to set yourself up as a furniture restorer. Similarly, if mathematics isn't your strong point you would probably be better off avoiding an accountancy franchise.

Play to your strengths: if you have previous experience in sales or marketing or management, look for a franchise that will put those skills to use. If you are good with your hands, consider franchises that require manual dexterity. And don't forget hobbies and interests: you may be a keen gardener, in which case an 'interior landscaping' business might appeal to you; or you may enjoy design, in which case a computer signage franchise could be right for you. (A word of warning, however: taking up a franchise is a hard-headed business decision – no matter how much the work appeals to you in terms of fulfilling some personal interest or enthusiasm, unless it generates sufficient income for you and your family, it's best forgotten.)

In general terms, franchised businesses have a lot in common. Without exception they require a sound understanding of quality and customer service. Newcomers to franchising bring valuable attributes from their experience in almost any sphere of employment. Whether you've worked in engineering, retailing, the police force or the social services, you will have acquired skills and knowledge that can be applied in just about any franchise. You may be surprised to find how broad your options are.

As a first step, rule out the areas that definitely do not appeal to you or for which you are unsuited. That may seem obvious advice but it's surprising how many people are tempted into thinking only of the money. An adequate financial return is of course vital, but so too is the non-material satisfaction to be gained from running the business – remember you're going to be working perhaps 40 or 50 hours a week, probably without holidays, and so you'd better enjoy it.

So you've brushed aside the stuff you simply couldn't face doing. Now you can take a positive, leisurely (there's no hurry) look at the options that might appeal to you. If, as you browse, you can picture yourself behind the bar of a pub, or helping people plan and book their holidays, or teaching children to sing and dance, or refitting kitchens, and you think, 'I wouldn't mind doing that', you are narrowing your choices almost without knowing it. It may turn out that one or other option isn't for you after all, but these are early days and there's no harm in sending off for some more information.

But we are running ahead of ourselves. First we must find out where to start the search.

Where to look

The British Franchise Association

Without doubt the first port of call should be the British Franchise Association (BFA). Founded in 1977 by eight companies,[1] who were franchising in the UK at that time, the association set out with two main objectives: first, to act as a trade association to represent and promote the interests of the franchising industry, and secondly, to distance reputable franchising from the dodgy practice of pyramid selling,[2] which was very much in the news in the early 1970s.

The BFA has since grown into an organisation with 190 franchisor members encompassing some 13,000 businesses. Its principal activities are to vet companies before admitting them to membership; to represent the British franchising industry in dealings with government and overseas franchise organisations; and to provide information and education on the subject of franchising.

This is what the BFA says about itself: 'One of our main jobs is to help potential franchisees recognise the good, the bad and the ugly for what they are. Another is to help businesses involved in franchising to secure their own position amongst the 'good' operators.

---

1. Prontoprint, Dyno-Rod, Wimpy International, Kentucky Fried Chicken, Budget Rent a Car, ServiceMaster, Ziebart Mobile Transport Services and Holiday Inns.
2. Pyramid selling involves paying a fee for the right to distribute a product. The aim, however, is not to build a bona fide distribution network but to make money from collecting initial fees. Existing distributors recruit more distributors and so the pyramid rises – and is built on sand.

'This work is not just a philanthropic exercise for reputable and responsible franchisors. It makes good commercial sense. The ability of franchisors to attract potential franchisees to invest in their systems depends crucially on their own reputation, and on the reputation of franchising in general.'

Membership criteria

The BFA operates a dual membership system comprising full and associate members. Its criteria demand that all members, full and associate, meet the following four general objectives:

1. **Viable.** All members of the BFA will have proved in the marketplace that their product or service is saleable, and furthermore saleable at a profit that will support a franchised network.
2. **Franchisable.** All members of the BFA will have proven they have the means to transfer their know-how to a new operator at arm's length. Most will have done so at their own risk through at least one managed pilot franchise operation.
3. **Ethical.** The BFA has joined with its sister bodies in Europe to devise a new and expanded code of ethics which all members commit themselves to abide by. The code requires standards of conduct in advertising, recruiting and selecting franchisees, and sets minimum conditions for the terms of franchise agreements. Those terms are both critical and complex.
4. **Disclosure.** All BFA members agree that they will disclose to prospective franchisees, in advance of any lasting contractual agreement and without ambiguity, the information on their business that is material to the franchise agreement. Members submit their offer documents to the association as part of the accreditation procedure.

Types of membership

Associate membership. With these checks on viability, franchisability, ethical and disclosed conduct in place, franchisors can be admitted to associate membership of the BFA, provided also that they commit themselves to abide by the Advertising Standards Authority's code of practice and also to the association's own complaints, disciplinary, appeals and re-accreditation rules.

Full membership. To become full members, franchisors must meet one more objective: they must have a proven trading and franchising record. The length of time a franchised business has been in operation, and the changes in business and financial circumstances it must have survived before it can be said to be 'established' will vary from sector to sector. The record of full members on openings, withdrawals, and failures (if any), as well as their trading and financial performance, is subject to an initial assessment and periodic checks.

New entrants and provisional listing. Just because a franchise proposition is new it does not mean that it is necessarily bad – though it may be. The association, therefore, introduced in 1991 a provisional list for the companies new to franchising who can nevertheless demonstrate that they are taking all reasonable measures to make sure that their business is properly developed and tested for the franchise method.

Professional affiliates. The BFA's membership criteria have been the subject of consultation with the professional advisers affiliated to the BFA, who provide legal, accountancy, banking and other services. The advice of those who are expert, not only in their own field, but also in franchising is vital. Here is another job for the BFA – accrediting the franchise knowledge and experience of its professional affiliates.

Taken together, the BFA's vetting procedures and the code of ethics it requires member companies to abide by are the nearest thing to a guarantee that a prospective franchisee is likely to find. It does not follow that success is assured: as we have seen even the most reputable franchised business can make mistakes, particularly when it comes to recruitment. But as a general rule if you pick a BFA member you start off at an advantage.

That said, BFA membership accounts for less than one third of all the franchised businesses identified in the association's annual survey of the industry, so to confine your search to the BFA is to reduce your options considerably. We are therefore left with something of a conundrum. On the one hand, it is fair to say that there are perfectly sound franchises that choose to remain outside the BFA. On the other, it would be nice to know why. Don't they want to pay the subscription? Don't they like the idea of a code of ethics? Don't they want to disclose full information about themselves? Whatever the answer, there must always be the suspicion that they have something to hide. So if you are interested in a non-member franchise, there is nothing for it, you're going to have to try and apply the same criteria that the BFA uses, which means doing a lot more investigative work and asking a lot more questions. We'll tell you how in the next chapter.

Other sources of information

Still with the BFA, another source of information is their **Franchisee's Information Pack,** which includes: a full list of member companies, what they do, contact details, and investment costs; a list of affiliate advisers; details of the BFA's role in franchising; and a copy of a video, *Your Introduction to Franchising*.

Seminars

The BFA runs a series of **Franchisee Seminars** across the country in partnership with Business Link Hertfordshire, and, in Scotland with Forth Valley Enterprise and Scottish Enterprise. 'The seminars,' says the association, 'consist of a series of balanced presentations delivered by speakers with practical experience of franchising. Full of relevant case studies, they highlight best practice and help you to identify the potential problems and pitfalls of franchising.'

Exhibitions

The **British Franchise Exhibitions,** organised by Venture Marketing Group and backed by the BFA, are an opportunity to see a selection of franchise companies at close range and talk to the people involved. There are four shows each year, in Manchester, London, Glasgow and Birmingham. The largest of these is the autumn National Franchise Exhibition at the National Exhibition Centre in Birmingham. In recent years this show has been the highlight of National Franchise Week, a seven-day programme of events across the country organised by the BFA to spread the word about business format franchising.

All the exhibitions feature a programme of seminars for prospective franchisees that visitors can attend at no extra charge. There is also an opportunity to meet independent franchise experts, such as lawyers, accountants, franchise consultants and bankers, and pick their brains. A major attraction of the exhibition programme is that every franchise company exhibiting has been approved by the BFA and is actively looking for new franchisees.

Before attending an exhibition it is advisable to obtain in advance a list of exhibitors, pick out those that most interest you, and do your homework. Exhibitions can be exhausting occasions. By going prepared you can get the most out them and minimise what they'll take out of you.

Literature

Other sources of information include **newspapers, magazines and Web sites.** Several national newspapers, notably the *Daily Express*, carry regular features on franchising opportunities. Among the specialist journals *Business Franchise Magazine* offers a brightly written combination of news and feature articles, as does *Franchise World*. There are dozens of Web sites devoted to franchising, including the BFA's at www.british-franchise.org. Some others are listed in Appendix IV.

Setting your financial targets

As you investigate the opportunities you will see that the required investments vary considerably, from less than £10,000 for a van-based franchise with few overheads to half a million or more for a high street fast food restaurant. When you buy a franchise you incur all the costs that you expect in setting up any business – leases, fixtures and fittings, stock, working capital and so on. But on top of that, as we have noted, franchisees pay the franchisor in two ways: first through an initial fee and then through regular payments for the duration of the contract. Before deciding how much you can afford, it's worth looking a little more closely at how the payment system works.

The initial franchise fee

In theory, and indeed quite often in practice, the initial franchise fee is to pay for costs incurred by the franchisor in setting up the new franchisee's outlet. These include:

- finding a suitable area and site;
- training;
- operations manual;
- help with recruiting and training staff where applicable;
- advertising and public relations and promotional launch;
- professional fees and legal costs;
- possibly the down-payment on a van;
- tools and equipment.

The picture, however, may be slightly more complicated than that. When a franchisor launches his business he is bound to have an idea of how much it is going to cost to develop the network and how many franchisees he can reasonably expect to recruit. Since his aim will be to recover the cost by selling the franchises, he will have a notional idea of the appropriate initial fee. He must, however, proceed with caution because in respectable franchising circles it is generally held to be very bad form to make a profit from initial fees. There are sound reasons for that: first, hefty initial fees could unduly hamper the franchisee's business in its tender early years, and, second, reputable franchisors want to distance themselves as far as possible from shady operators whose aim is to make money purely from selling so-called franchises.

Because of concerns such as these, franchisors seldom seek to recover all of their setting-up costs (which will include items such as developing the system, pilot testing and trade mark registration) by loading the initial fee. Even so, it is reasonable to assume that the franchisor will include an element of those set-up costs in the initial fees in addition to the costs incurred in establishing the franchisee in business.

In some ways it's a difficult balancing act: if a franchisor sets the initial fees too high, it may hamper recruitment; if he sets them too low, they will be insufficient to recover the costs of setting up new outlets. Also, in the early days when there are only a few outlets, the income from management services fees may be insufficient to generate a profit for the franchisor. It is important, therefore, that a franchisor has enough capital to see the business safely through its early stages. It is a great help if the pilot operations are providing revenue through this potentially difficult period.

But whatever the arguments for and against high initial fees, it is now generally accepted that the initial franchise fee should not be more than 10 per cent of the franchisee's total starting-up costs (though this varies according to the type of franchise: a van-based operation, say, at the cheaper end of the investment scale, may require a larger percentage of the total in initial fees). It is also accepted that the franchisor's main source of income should be in the form of management services fees. This has the effect both of keeping the initial franchise fee down and encouraging the franchisor to stay on his toes to justify the regular payments he demands.

Other regular payments

Although an income from management fees rewards the franchisor for his enterprise in setting up the organisation, it has another purpose, which is to make a contribution towards his central overheads and to cover his costs in providing continuing management advice and support. He uses this income to fund items such as support staff, marketing and public relations, research and development, and continuing training of franchisees and their staff. The aim should always be to provide an adequate level of support and to set fee levels that allow a fair return to both franchisor and franchisee. The franchisees should be satisfied that, in return for their regular fee payments, the franchisor is providing them with the kind of support and services that they could not provide for themselves, such as research and development and the negotiating of national contracts.

There are three kinds of regular payments that may be made to the franchisor:

- a percentage on turnover;
- a mark-up on materials bought from the franchisor; and
- a regular fixed amount.

Of these, the percentage on turnover, or management services fee, is by far the most common.

Management services fees

In the interests of fairness, it is customary for every franchisee in the network to pay the same percentage of turnover. Therefore, before selling franchises, the franchisor must decide what an appropriate level of fee should be. The pilot operation should provide essential information on the likely sales and returns from an average outlet and therefore guide the franchisor in setting a fair fee. Though the percentage varies from franchise to franchise and from sector to sector, as a rough guide the management services fee is usually about 10 per cent of turnover and a franchisee can expect to hand over perhaps 20 or even 30 per cent of his annual trading profit to the franchisor in the shape of management services fees. So you can see why franchisees expect something meaningful in return. (From the franchisor's point of view, fees levied on turnover have the additional advantage of allowing him access to the franchisees' sales records, an important aid to keeping track of individual performance.)

Mark-ups and commissions

The second method of charging franchisees is to require them to buy some or all of their materials and supplies from the franchisor or from a nominated supplier. The franchisor gets his money by charging a mark-up or getting a commission from the nominated supplier.

Whether regular charges come in the shape of management fees or mark-ups, they are a potential source of difficulty. It is easy to see how a franchisee may quickly come to resent writing a large monthly cheque payable to the franchisor. For his part, the franchisor may have difficulty in checking the accuracy of the figures provided to him by the franchisees. Mark-ups overcome this problem, but only in part – although the franchisor gets his slice of the action by selling materials to his franchise network, there is always the possibility that some franchisees may avoid the mark-up by buying cheaper supplies from alternative sources. If that happens, there is the danger that inferior materials might compromise the quality of the finished product. The mark-up system also carries the risk that franchisees might nurture suspicious thoughts about the fairness of being tied to a single supplier and charged a percentage, the precise size of which may not be disclosed. Though neither system is perfect, the management fee is more transparent and therefore much more widely used.

Regular fixed payments

A third possibility, charging a fixed fee, is seldom used, mainly because it could prove too onerous a burden for the franchisee in the early days, but also because the franchisor stands to lose out if the franchised outlets successfully build up their turnovers in succeeding years.

Advertising levies

One more form of regular payment may be required by the franchisor and that is an advertising levy. This may be about five per cent of turnover and is used to cover the cost of national advertising and promotion.

Calculating your personal net worth

To sum up, your investment in a franchise will comprise the normal costs of setting up a business (working capital,[3] plant and equipment, staff recruitment, professional fees, and so on) plus an initial fee. With that in mind, you must now work out roughly (since it is unlikely that you will reach a precise figure) how much you can afford to invest.

As a first step calculate the figure known in financial circles as your net worth. Your net worth is the difference between what you own and what you owe. In other words, your net worth is your **assets** minus your **liabilities**. If you have more assets than liabilities, you have a positive net worth. If you have more liabilities than assets, you have a negative net worth. Draw up a two column list with your assets – your house, car, investments and so on – on one side, and your liabilities – mortgage, credit card debts and so on – on the other side. Add up the figures in each column and deduct your liabilities from your assets. All being well, the result will be a positive sum, the size of which will give an indication of the amount you will be able to invest in a franchise. It is not, however, quite as simple as that. On the downside, net worth, though important, is not in itself a sufficient guide; you will need to make an assessment of your liquid assets, ie cash or other items that can quite readily be converted into cash. On the upside, most sound franchise companies have arrangements with the high street banks allowing you to borrow money to invest. As a rough guide they will lend up to three times your liquid funds. Seen in that light, your target figure should look a lot more attainable.

Location

A final point worth considering at this stage is your willingness to uproot yourself and your family and move to where the opportunity is. One of

---

3. A key component, which is often overlooked. A new franchisee will need sufficient working capital to see him or her through the early stages until the business is profitable.

the great merits of franchising is the local knowledge that franchisees bring to the network, and ideally each new franchisee will set up shop in his or her home town. That is most likely to happen when a franchised business is in its early stages and the network is just getting established. If, however, the franchise of your choice is well-established, or well on the way to being established, there may already be a franchisee operating in your locality. You then face a tough decision: either to look for a different franchise opportunity – the second choice on your list perhaps – or to up sticks and move to another part of the country where a territory is available.

Factors to consider will be ties to your locality, such as schooling, and the state of the housing market. Though it may make sound business sense to relocate, the disruption will undoubtedly add extra strain to the already stressful move into self-employment. Then again, the whole aim of going into franchising is to better yourself and to enhance your income, and if a move to a different area opens the way to a better business opportunity than can be found near you, the benefits in the medium- to long-term should outweigh the short-term trials of the upheaval. As the tiresome old phrase has it, only you can decide.

Setting the ball rolling

Once your initial search is complete you will probably have narrowed down your choice to two or three sectors that appeal to you. They could, for example, be cleaning, fast food and quick printing, all successful areas for franchising and each comprising a number of companies. Your research will have told you who they are, so now is the time to write, telephone, or go to their Web sites and ask to be sent some information.

6
Snooping and sleuthing

Investigating the business opportunity

They come through the letterbox day after day, thudding heavily on the doormat, brochure after brochure, all extolling the franchises they offer, some masterpieces of the graphic designer's art, others looking more like the work of a hard-pressed amateur. Unless you have already met a few franchisors at an exhibition or seminar, these – usually glossy – leaflets and booklets are your first contact with the company that may come to play a huge part in your life. Look through them carefully. Of course, they will be persuasive – this is, after all, promotional literature – but are they also informative? Is what you are reading just a hard sell and few facts, or is it a serious attempt to explain what the company does, the market in which it operates, and what it expects of its franchisees? Does it give a clear indication of the required investment? Does it provide a checklist of questions to ask yourself? In short, does it give the impression of professionalism, of an organisation that is both experienced and knowledgeable?

Promotional literature comes in a variety of shapes and sizes, from the shiny, colour-printed and lavishly-illustrated to the photocopied sheet. First impressions are important, but not everything. It is not unheard of for conmen whose aim is to make a quick killing to produce very impressive-looking brochures – they might well constitute their single biggest outlay – designed purely to snare the unwary. On the other hand, a genuine business with real potential might let itself down by skimping on its brochure. Be suspicious of the two extremes: if a franchise has obviously gone to considerable expense to produce promotional literature that strikes you as 'flashy' rather than informative, watch out for the hard sell; if you are sent a badly-typed, misspelt sheet of paper (not unknown, believe it or not) send it winging into the wastepaper bin.

Assuming you like what you see and are tempted to take matters further, your investigations must now begin in earnest. These entail firstly looking at the industry in which the franchise operates and – assuming the answers are encouraging – moving on to look at the franchise company itself. Evaluating a franchise is a time-consuming and painstaking task. It has to be. Buying a franchise is a serious business that can have a profound effect on your life, either for good or ill. You must, to the best of your ability, learn what you are letting yourself in for. Once the agreement is signed, there is no going back, and there's nothing worse than discovering that a bad mistake could have been avoided if only you had known more before you put your name on the dotted line.

There is no other way to find out what you need to know than to ask a lot of questions. Don't be afraid to give a franchisor a polite grilling. If he is genuine, he should have nothing to hide, and in any case it is as much in his interest as yours that all the relevant facts are made plain. Franchising is a partnership between the franchisee and the franchisor, and if it is to succeed it obviously makes sense that both parties to the agreement understand fully what is involved. Nor will you confine your questioning to the franchisor: as your investigations proceed, you will also talk to lawyers, accountants, bankers, the BFA, and existing franchisees. That way you will build up as complete a picture as possible and give yourself the best chance of making the right decision and perhaps, just as important, avoiding the wrong decision.

Begin with a broad brush

So let us start with a broad assessment of the area that interests you. Franchising is most successful when the following conditions are met:

- The market for the product or service is buoyant.
- The product or service cannot easily be copied by others.

- It is not a passing fad or fashion.
- There is not much in the way of competition. Better still, there is no competition at all.
- The demand for the product is not price sensitive.
- The product or service is using some special technology or system that works better than traditional methods.

Products and services

These are the kind of questions you should be asking about the products and services:

- Is the market growing? Is it static? Or is it declining?
- Does the product or service enjoy a repeat business?
- Does the product or service have any special features to make it attractive to buyers?
- Is there much competition? Is the franchise in which you are interested well-established in the industry or a relative newcomer?
- Does the product or service justify a premium price?
- Is there already strong public awareness of the product or service?
- Is the product or service protected by trade marks or patents?
- Do you see advertisements for the product or service? Do you know of people who are buying or using the product or service?

These questions are designed to find out whether the product or service can be sold to a sufficiently large market and at a sufficiently large price. As we have seen, for a franchise to succeed it is essential it should generate enough profit for both the franchisee and the franchisor, as well as providing customer satisfaction. To achieve that, the product must have genuine advantages over the competition and should not lend itself to copying. If the only real difference between the product or service and what is offered by the competition comes down to packaging and presentation, that is unlikely to be sufficient to sustain a long-term advantage. Look for qualities more substantial than that.

Investigating the franchise

Although the ideal franchise will have a unique product or service that is not supplied by anyone else, in reality that is so rare as to be almost non-existent. As a franchisee you are likely to face competition. In meeting it – and beating it – you will rely on providing better quality and service. In some cases you may be able to offer better prices, but usually your competitive edge will be in delivery.

Just as important as sufficient demand in the marketplace is the efficiency and quality of the franchise that you are operating. The long-term success of a franchise operation rests on its systems and the support it gives to its franchisees. And that, in turn, comes down to marketing programmes, administrative systems, training, and research and development. So the second stage of your appraisal involves looking closely at the franchise.

What you are trying to discover at this stage is whether it was pilot-tested; the quality and extent of support you are likely to get from the franchisor; the quality and extent of the training you will be given; whether existing franchisees are satisfied; whether the business will provide the kind of return you're looking for; and whether it is financially sound.

To get a general picture of the financial strength and standing of a franchised business you can gather information from Companies House, the BFA, and perhaps from a company search, which you can commission for a fee from a specialist service company (the internet can be a help here). If any of these inquiries unearths something that makes you suspicious, you should retreat at this early stage. (See Appendix I for a brief guide to interpreting reports and accounts.) Though bogus franchises are not usually difficult to sniff out, they can do a lot of harm – people have lost their life's savings – and the best advice is, if in doubt get out. There will be plenty of other franchises to look at.

The franchise interview

By now you will probably have narrowed down your selection to two or three franchise companies that have come out well in your preliminary inquires. The next stage is the interview. It is important that you should approach this as a meeting of adults on equal terms. You are not going along as a job applicant. You are going to discuss a possible business partnership. So while the franchisor will want to satisfy himself that you will be an asset to his business, you will want to know about him.

General questions

Here are the key questions you should ask.

- **Is the franchise a member of the BFA?** If so, what category of member? Membership is a definite plus point.
- **How experienced is the franchisor?** How many outlets are company-owned? How well established is the franchise network? The fewer the number of existing outlets, the greater will be the risk for a new franchisee. You will need to weigh that up in making your final decision. Your previous experience in, say, marketing or management may equip you to handle extra risk.
- **Is the franchisor financially sound?** Your earlier research at Companies House or elsewhere should have given you an idea of the answer, but now is your chance to ask for confirmation and/or further information. Ask to see reports and accounts for the last three years. In the case of a newer company, ask for a banker's status report. At a later stage your accountant or bank may want to take up references: no reputable franchisor should have any objection to this.
- **Ask about the training you will be given**. How long does it last? Where will it take place? At a training centre, in the field, or both? Is the training both initial and ongoing? What does it cover? Will you be trained not only in product knowledge and how to deliver the product or service but also in more general areas such as business administration, marketing, and staff recruitment?
- **How much support will you be given once you get started?** Does the franchisor's head office team have sufficient experience and resources to give you help when you need it? Is there a head office sales team

beavering away to get new business for franchisees? If, as is likely, you are expected to generate some or all of your own sales, how much help will you get in the shape of promotional materials? Ask to see samples. Do they impress you? Will you be given sales help and support in the field?

- **Ask about expansion plans over the next five years.** Has the franchisor set a target for the total number of franchised outlets he wants in the network? How quickly is he planning to proceed? Are there plans to step up head office support to keep pace with expansion plans or does the franchisor consider the existing arrangements sufficient to cope? If the franchise is well established, what is the franchisor doing to keep ahead of the competition? Is he still keen to develop and refine the system? Can he show you evidence of this?
- **How are franchisees selected?** What qualities are sought? What previous experience, if any, is required? What kind of backgrounds do existing franchisees come from? How many failures have there been?

Financial questions

Next we come to questions that are specifically financial.

- **What is the initial fee?** What is the management service fee? How do these compare with other franchises? (The BFA and your bank manager should be able to help with this last question.) What is the advertising contribution?
- What are the **financial projections** for the outlet that you will be starting up? How were they arrived at? Are they realistic?
- Will the **forecast income** for the first year or so be sufficient to meet your current commitments?
- Will the **projected profit** be sufficient in the medium to long-term to (a) meet your expectations and (b) to fund further growth of the business?
- **Where will you obtain your supplies** of goods and raw materials? Will the franchisor be the sole source?

- Has the franchisor arranged a finance package with the Big Four banks? (See Chapter 9.)

Contractual questions

Now for questions relating to the terms of the agreement. Ask to take home a copy of the Franchise Agreement to look through at your leisure. The key things you will be looking for are:

- Will you be operating in an **exclusive territory**?
- **How long does the contract run?** Is it renewable without payment of a further fee?
- How free will you be to **assign or sell** the franchise?

Reviewing the situation

With the interview done, you can mull over what you have learnt and think over the impressions you have come away with. Did the franchisor strike you as someone who knows his stuff? Was he enthusiastic about his business in particular and about franchising in general? Did you get the impression that he was open and honest, or did he at times strike you as evasive?

Did he come across as the sort of person you could get on with? Did he seem over-keen to recruit you? If so, be wary. A good franchisor is very selective about the franchisees he chooses; someone who wants to make a quick killing will take on anyone provided they come up with the money. Similarly, if the franchisor seemed unduly gung-ho and optimistic about expansion, this is a bad sign. While all franchisors want to grow their businesses, the best proceed in a measured way, taking pains to be sure they have sufficient resources to support an expanding network.

Was the franchisor cagey about the financial side of the operation? One can understand a business wanting to maintain confidentiality about certain aspects of its affairs, but as a prospective partner you want clear investment information from the start. The more open the franchisor the greater will be your confidence in him.

Now you have been close to the operation and met one or more of the people running it, it's a good idea to go over again in your mind the answers to some of the key questions raised earlier in this book. On reflection, do you still think you would be happy running the business? Do you feel in your heart that there is a market in your area for what you will be selling?

Talking of selling, would you be any good at it? It is human nature to want to be liked. No one likes to be rejected, which probably explains why most people are not cut out for selling – they simply cannot bear the thought of being turned down or turned away. The amount of selling involved in a franchise varies from one operation to another. Some franchises, for example, will canvass on your behalf to help you get started and in the process show you how it is done. After that, though, you are likely to be left to drum up further business using your own effort and initiative. Even franchises that rely largely for their income on 'distress purchases' – emergency plumbing, for example – still require some selling – after all, it is down to the franchisee to make the market aware of his existence and the service he provides. It is, therefore, fair to say that in common with all other businesses the majority of franchises require some active selling on the part of the owner operator if the outlets are to achieve their full potential. Your willingness to go out and promote your business and your ability, if necessary, to develop a thick skin are matters to which you should give considerable thought.

Meeting existing franchisees

The next stage of the franchise appraisal should help you to resolve these issues and many more besides. It is essential – one cannot over-emphasise the importance of this – to meet at least two existing franchisees. There is no better way to find out what you are letting yourself in for than to talk to people who have been there already and are experiencing life at the coal-face. You will, however, need to keep your wits about you and make judgments about the people you are meeting before attaching too much importance to what they tell you.

As we have seen, franchising hinges on the relationship between the franchisor and the franchisee, and there can be faults on both sides. So if you meet a franchisee who is disaffected in some way, do not necessarily assume that the blame lies with the franchisor – the franchisee could have brought the difficulties on himself. That is why it is important to talk to several franchisees, preferably from differing backgrounds and with varying degrees of experience, and why you must make your own assessment of their character and ability. We'll come back to this later.

In order to choose the franchisees whom you will meet you must of course get a list from the franchisor. Any open, honest reputable franchisor should have no problem with this. What you want is a complete list of *all* the existing franchisees in the network, not the names of a select few chosen by the franchisor. If there is a reluctance to let you have this information, ask yourself why and feel free to draw your own conclusions. When you have chosen the franchisees you wish to meet, make appointments to see them, and go along on your own or with your partner. You should resist any attempt by the franchisor to tag along at these meetings since his presence is likely to have an inhibiting affect on the franchisees.

There are lots of questions to ask but they are all directed to finding the answers to just two: 'Are you happy running the franchise?' and 'Are you making as much money as you hoped?' It's obvious when you think about it: you go into business for two main reasons – job satisfaction and profit. As Gordon Gekko, the rapacious stock trader in the film *Wall Street*, said, 'It's all about bucks, kid. All the rest is conversation.' Though I couldn't possibly endorse such a blindingly mercenary sentiment, the British have a tendency to err in the other direction and become coy when asked about money, particularly how much they earn. But when meeting franchisees, you must take this particular conversational hurdle in your stride.

Money matters

Ask if they are making the profit that was forecast and, if not, why not? Are there any particular factors that affect the profitability of the business? Ask about cashflow. Is it a problem? (This is a key point because cash is the lifeblood of a business; if there is a suggestion of a difficulty you should investigate this further, find out if other franchisees have similar problems, and, if so, take it up with the franchisor.)

Ask about the franchisees' investment in the business. Was the actual cost the same as that advertised or were there any hidden extras? Ask whether the sales targets were realistic. Have they been met? If not, why not? Are supplies delivered promptly? Is advertising carried out by the franchisor? How easy has it been to attract customers? How much selling is involved?

Relationships

Now make some inquiries about how the franchise relationship has turned out in practice. What is the franchisor like to work with? Is he approachable and fair-minded? Is support there when it's needed? Ask about training. Was it thorough? How long did it last? Are the operations manuals helpful and easy to follow?

Morale

Try to get a sense of the morale among franchisees. Ask if they enjoy running their business. Ask whether it has come up to their expectations. Given the chance, would they do it all over again? Has the business meant any changes to their family life? What are the best things about running the franchise? And the worst? Do they know of any franchise failures in the company? If so, what went wrong? Do they scrupulously follow the systems laid down by the franchisor or are they inclined to go their own way?

Next steps

The responses to these questions should reveal not only many of the things you need to know about the practicality of running the franchise but also the nature of the people you have been questioning. You will have formed an opinion as to whether they were businesslike, hard working, efficient, and interested in providing a quality service to their customers. Were they personable? Did you like them? Can you picture yourself being members of the same club as them? How did their experience and background equip them for running the franchise? How do their backgrounds compare with your own?

As we have seen already, very few franchises are based on a truly original concept or product; what makes them work is that they have been packaged into a system that can easily be replicated and followed. When you buy a franchise you are, above all, buying a system. It follows that the closer you stick to the tried and tested formula, the greater are your chances of getting the rewards that you want. So if any of the franchisees you've met have not been doing as well as they had hoped, try to establish how closely they have been following the systems. It may be that in deviating from the path laid down by the franchisor, they have been the author of their own misfortune. It would be a mistake to turn down a good franchise because of the experiences of bad franchisees. If, however, they have done everything by the book and are still dissatisfied, is that because, in your judgment, they are perhaps not suited by either temperament or disposition to be franchisees? Or does it seem to you that their experience suggests the franchise might not be all that it is cracked up to be? The answers to those questions, combined with the results of your earlier research, should determine whether or not you strike a particular franchise off your list.

7
The crunch: individual investment opportunities

By now you will have assessed your own strengths and weaknesses, looked at your finances, read magazines and newspapers, tramped around exhibitions, gathered together lots of information about various franchises, narrowed down your choice – first to two or three sectors and then to two or three companies, investigated those companies in more detail, spoken to existing franchisees, and probably thought about taking a long holiday or calling for an ambulance. But don't. There's still plenty more to do before you can throw open the doors of your very own business and start trading, and this is no time to weaken. In any case you are now at the exciting stage of investigating the actual business that you could be running – what began as a dream is getting ever closer to reality. Remember, however, that this is still an investigation.

Having put in all that hard work, there is a temptation to get carried away at this stage and lose your sense of objectivity. This must be resisted at all costs. However appealing a particular outlet may seem, it has to be looked at thoroughly long before you sign on the dotted line. And not just by you. You have reached the point where you will need to call in expert help and advice.

Location, location, location

But first, where is your business going to be? Just as the three most important factors in determining the value of a house are location, location, and location, so too are they essential in influencing the success of a business. Ideally, you want to set up in your own locality, or at least in a location within easy reach of your home. In this, as in many other aspects of opening your outlet, the franchisor's assistance will be invaluable. He will tell you whether there is an opportunity close to you. If, however, that particular territory has already been allocated, he will suggest the nearest alternative. Go and look at the area. Find out more about it. The aim is to assess its potential.

You will already know about the product or service and the kind of market at which is it aimed. Is the area that you are being offered any different from the market in general, or does it seem to you to be well suited to the business? For example, if you are planning to provide a business-to-business service such as quick print are there plenty of potential small business customers within easy reach? Or if your product or service is premium-priced (and many franchised products or services are), is the area sufficiently prosperous to provide you with a good profit?

Look, too, at the size of the territory you are being offered. Is it big enough to provide you with sufficient customers? The franchisor should have investigated the market potential and ought to be able to provide you with figures such as local demographics. It is increasingly common for franchisors to allocate postcode territories to new franchisees, which is a convenient and easy way to draw the boundaries and offer a market with sufficient potential.

Look at the competition in the territory. Are there many other businesses offering a similar service, just a few, or none at all? (*Yellow Pages* and advertisements in local newspapers are good sources of information.) Do you think your franchise – what it offers, the way it looks, the way you plan to run it – will offer something new or different that will make it stand out from the competition?

Home-based franchises

Many franchises, usually at the lower end of the investment scale, allow franchisees to start their businesses from home. This has the obvious advantage of cutting down overheads – no extra rents, rates or service charges. There may, however, be disadvantages. Working from home might not fit well into family life, especially if there are young children about, or the house is small. When your home is your workplace it is more difficult to shut off the cares of the day when, at last, you finish.

You may also get into difficulties with your neighbours or the local authority if the nature of your work brings extra traffic into the neighbourhood or causes noise or disruption in some other way. The best policy is to keep a low profile. In this, however, as in many respects, the prospective franchisee has an advantage over people starting up on their own. Unlike them, you will have the franchisor's knowledge and experience behind you. He will know if there are any possible problems associated with operating the business from home and will be able to offer advice on avoiding them. In most cases there ought to be no difficulty.

Home-based franchisees tend to be either 'white collar workers' offering, say, accountancy services, or people running a mobile franchise, in which case home is just a base. Either way, it is not unusual for a franchisee to start off the business from home and later, when the customer base has expanded, to move to business premises, take on staff, and adopt a more managerial role.

Retail outlets

If you are going to operate from a retail outlet special considerations apply. Here location really is everything. There are primary and secondary locations and, naturally the former cost a lot more than the latter. Primary locations are smack bang in the high street where there is plenty of passing trade. Secondary locations are up the side streets where the customers will need to seek you out. Your choice depends on the nature of the business. If you are running a fast food restaurant you will want to be accessible to the maximum number of customers. If, on the other hand, you are offering, say, a picture framing service, your customers will, thanks to your marketing efforts and your growing reputation, make the effort to come to you, in which case a secondary location ought not to be a disadvantage: it will certainly be less expensive and you should have a longer list of premises from which to choose.

Buying an existing franchise

It is a common mistake among prospective franchisees to assume that they must inevitably start from scratch – seeking out premises, equipping them, stocking up, and then embarking on the nerve-wracking process of finding customers. But there is another way: you might be able to buy an existing franchise. The advantages are obvious – in return for your investment you still get the training needed to run the business and the support you need to make it work, but on top of that you will be getting the goodwill bound up in an existing business, a ready-made customer base, and an immediate cashflow.

A franchise re-sale, or 'business transfer' as it is known, will almost certainly require a larger investment than a franchised outlet started from scratch, but you may consider the benefits to be worth that extra outlay. You will want to know, of course, why the existing franchisee is selling the business. The most common reason is that he or she is retiring. Other possibilities include ill health, a desire to move on and do something different, or a simple urge to cash in and realise the capital that the owner has painstakingly built up in the business.

There is another possibility – that the franchisee has been unable to make a successful go of it. If that is the case you will need to probe further. What went wrong? Was the lack of success down to the franchisee (a lack of drive, a lack of interest, a weak approach to selling) or, more worryingly, was it to do with the local market? Was the catchment area too small? Was the business location wrong? Was it difficult to find suitable staff? The franchisor will have his own ideas why the outlet's potential was not fully realised, and you should listen to those. But in the end you will have to make your own judgment about the outlet and the people who were running it.

To help you assess an existing franchise you should be given access to the past accounts of the business. Ask to see the books for at least the last three years and pass them on to your accountant for strict scrutiny. The accounts of a small business need to be looked at with an expert eye because they are not necessarily audited. They were probably prepared purely for tax purposes and might therefore provide not much more than a bare statement of sales and expenses, rather than a reliable guide to past performance. Your accountant will know what to look for and should be able to advise you on any points that might have affected the performance of the business.

If you get the impression that the business has unfulfilled potential, do you think you could do better and if so, why? Do you think you could beef up sales? Do you think your personality and drive could make a difference? Don't be modest. Just be honest.

This matter of sales is vital to any business but assumes a special significance with a franchised outlet. With a traditional business transfer, ie an unfranchised outlet, the new owner has three main ways to increase profits – by cutting costs, putting up prices, or selling more. With a franchise, the first two options may be out of the hands of the franchisee or available only in a limited way. So his or her ability to drive up sales becomes the single most powerful means of making a difference and improving performance.

Starting afresh

Assuming there is no existing franchise for sale, or at any rate not one that appeals to you, and you opt instead to start a brand new outlet, you will still need to have some sort of financial information to go on. Your franchisor should provide you with a sample business plan and estimated profit and loss accounts, based on the performance of his pilot operations and that of existing franchised outlets. These will be a guide to the kind of costs and income you can expect but they are not in any sense a guarantee of success.

So much will depend on the way you run the business (how closely you stick to the systems, how much energy you bring to the operation) and on local conditions that forecasts are, of necessity, no more than rough guides. However, it is not at all uncommon for new franchisees to declare triumphantly that they have reached their targets ahead of time, sometimes by as much as a year, which suggests that some franchisors wisely err on the side of caution when drawing up projections. Though it might be tempting to base predictions on the best-performing outlets in the network, it is far better to encourage more modest expectations, partly because they are more likely to be met and therefore be a powerful boost to the morale of new franchisee and also because a franchisor needs to build the support of the big banks and they do not take kindly to being misled by a series of bullish forecasts.

Show the sample business plan and estimated profit and loss accounts to your accountant, always assuming you have one, which brings us to the essential matter of consulting experts.

Seeking professional advice

Now that you have reached the critical stage of buying a franchise – the point at which the franchisor is presenting you with financial projections and a legal document called a Franchise Agreement – you must secure the backing of team of expert advisers. In all probability the franchisor will be extremely helpful. He may take you step by step through the financial and legal points, explaining what is involved and how it will affect you. You may well come away from these meetings feeling confident and assured. But you still need to get expert impartial advice. It is always tempting to bypass this process, mainly because of the costs involved.

As everyone knows, solicitors and accountants do not come cheap. You will be looking at an outlay of several hundred pounds for a detailed assessment of the financial and legal ins and outs of what you may be letting yourself in for. What if, when all this poring over the documents is complete, your advisers shake a sorrowful head and pronounce the venture to which you have pinned so many hopes to be the dreaded lemon? You'll still have to pay their fees, so you end up out of pocket, with no franchise, and no choice but to start again. It's a gloomy prospect and might explain why a survey[1] found that only 25 per cent of a sample

---

1. Franchise Success – Perceptions and Barriers, Lloyds Bank plc and the International Franchise Research Centre.

of franchisees had sought guidance from accountants and only 5 per cent from lawyers. But professional advice taken ahead of signing (or not signing) on the dotted line should be seen as a form of insurance and the fees as a kind of premium. If the advice turns out to be unfavourable, yes, it will have cost money but that doesn't mean you have got nothing in return. On the contrary you may well have been spared financial loss, wasted effort and heartache. Seen in that light, it's money well spent.

In any case, such a devastating verdict is improbable. Thanks to all the research and preparation you have put in, your chosen franchise is unlikely to be either fraudulent or hopelessly inadequate. What your advisers will be looking for are over-optimism in the financial projections and imperfections in the legal documents. An accountant will advise on matters such as the feasibility of turnover and profit projections, how much you should pay for the outlet, how best to raise the finance, and how to minimise your tax liability. He or she will help you to assess your own financial position and assist in preparing your presentation to the bank. A solicitor will go through the franchise agreement, explain the legal obligations you will be undertaking, and spot any difficulties: this process is well worthwhile since any errors, anomalies or misunderstandings could prove costly at a later date.

Specialist advisers

When choosing advisers, you should bear in mind that not any old solicitor or accountant will do. Franchising is a specialised area of expertise and, although an increasing number of legal and accountancy firms are getting to hear of it, comparatively few can claim true familiarity with the subject. So be sure to pick people who have a proven record of dealing with franchises.

A good place to start is your bank. Although your branch manager may not know a great deal about franchising, he or she has almost instant access to someone who does. The big high street banks have specialised franchise departments, which have built up a considerable body of knowledge on the franchises available in the UK today. This information is freely available to the branch network. So not only should your local branch be able quickly to find out about the franchise you are considering, it should also be able to recommend a solicitor and accountant who are well versed in franchising.

Failing that, the BFA's list of affiliate members includes solicitors and chartered accountants who have demonstrated to the satisfaction of the association an understanding of the franchising system. If you choose one of the big firms of specialists, it may be that they will undertake to go over your financial projections and check your franchise agreement as a one-off service.

Once your franchise is up and running, a local accountant who understands small businesses but does not claim any highly-specialised knowledge of franchising, should nevertheless be able to provide the continuing expertise you need in preparing your accounts for tax purposes and so on. If there are any problems specifically related to franchising, you can always refer back to the larger firm of specialists. Your bank, too, should be an ever-ready source of help and advice on the financial side.

A final word on appointing advisers. As your business grows and develops you will continue to need their services from time to time. So try to appoint people who you feel you will be able to get on with. Look, too, for plain speakers – men and women who can talk to you about financial and legal matters in simple, clear English. And sort out the matter of fees right at the beginning: get a good idea what you are going to be charged and, for your part, be clear about the services that you want. These things are best put in writing.

Making the decision: a final checklist

You have almost reached the final hurdles (the next two chapters deal with the Franchise Agreement and the raising of finance), but before coiling yourself ready to spring, go over yet again what you have learned about yourself and the business you are think of buying and running. Here is a quick checklist:

- Is the franchise you have chosen something you would really enjoy doing? Are you confident you have what it takes to make a go of it? Is it suited to your skills and capabilities?
- Are you sure the financial commitments that you will be taking on won't over-stretch you?
- Is the business likely to generate enough profit to meet your expectations?
- Are you really willing to work all the hours that God sends and possibly some more besides?
- Do you fully accept the need to follow the systems?

Don't be rushed into making a decision. Once the franchisor has satisfied himself that you are a suitable candidate he will want you to make the final decision quite quickly. If you have followed the appraisal procedures outlined so far in this book you should be well-equipped to make that judgment. Even so, if you still have some doubts or points that you want to raise, don't hesitate to discuss them with your advisers or to go back to the franchisees you met and talk to them again.

Okay, if you are now satisfied, or as satisfied as you are ever likely to be, that you have found the right franchise, that you like the franchisor, and that this is where your future lies, it's time to press on to the next stage and take a detailed look at the franchise contract.

8
The large print and the small

The franchise contract

If all goes well and your business flourishes, the franchise agreement will lie undisturbed in a drawer for the duration of the contract between you and the franchisor. If so, that will be a measure of its success: the fact that neither party needs to have recourse to the terms and conditions laid down in the formal legal document strongly suggests that all is well in the relationship and that any disagreements can be dealt with amicably and informally. But the fact that the best franchise agreements are destined to lie dormant does not mean they are superfluous and can be dispensed with. Far from it. The franchise agreement is a vital document whose importance cannot be understated. It lays down the terms and conditions of the franchise and the detailed obligations of both parties.

There is no special legislation governing franchising in English law, which means that the terms set out in the contract are all that the parties have to go on in determining their relationship. Anything that is not in the contract is not part of the agreement: this is important because it means that any promises, financial forecasts, or undertakings given by the franchisor or his representatives have no legal validity if they are not there, in black and white, in the contract.

The franchise agreement has three main functions:

1. to set down in writing what is agreed between the two parties in order to avoid disputes at a later date;
2. to protect the franchisor's rights to his know-how, trade marks, secret methods and so on; and
3. to lay down the rules which both parties agree to play by.

It is important to stress that the agreement should be exactly the same for every franchisee in the network. This is both fair and practical. Fair because every franchisee should have the same basic opportunities, rights and obligations; practical because should it become known that some are treated more favourably than others, discontent and jealousy would quickly sweep through the system, prejudicing the success of the whole operation. So if it seems to you that the franchisor is offering you special terms or is willing to change the contract to suit your particular case, be extremely wary. It may be that he is desperate for a sale, always a bad sign, or that he is untrustworthy – if he's prepared to cut a deal for you, who's to say he isn't offering even better terms to someone else? A reputable franchisor will have worked out the terms of his contract to suit his business and with the help of legal advice. This really is a case of one size fits all, and if you feel unhappy with the terms laid down in the agreement and would like to change them, you would probably be better to forget that particular franchise and look elsewhere.

Franchise contracts differ from franchise to franchise in order to take into account the varying natures of the businesses; a contract for a mobile franchise will be different from that of a retail franchise, the terms for a fast food franchise will differ from those of a drain cleaning operation. That said, all franchise contracts tend to have features in common. So let's look at these in some detail.

Most franchise agreements come in two parts. The first is often described as the purchase agreement, the second as the franchise agreement.

The purchase agreement

In effect, the purchase agreement is a declaration of good faith on the part of both parties and a mutual undertaking to proceed to a full agreement provided certain conditions are met. In signing a purchase agreement you, the prospective franchisee, are saying, 'Yes, I like the look of this franchise and want to press ahead. Let's move on and see if you can find suitable premises (or in the case of a mobile franchise, help me find a vehicle) while I approach the banks and raise the finance.'

The purchase agreement is a loose one. It gives the franchisor the go-ahead to research the feasibility of the area in which you, the franchisee, intend to set up; to look for a suitable site; prepare cashflow projections; book you into the training programme; and check your references. You will have to pay over some money when you sign the purchase agreement to cover costs incurred by the franchisor in setting the ball rolling. However, if for any reason things don't work out at this stage – for instance, suitable premises may not be available within an agreed time period – either party might be able to back out of the agreement.

If the failure to meet the terms is caused by the franchisor's inability to find a suitable site, for example, or satisfy himself that the market area you have chosen is viable, you will probably be entitled to a full refund of your deposit. If on the other hand, you fail to reach agreement because you don't like what the franchisor is offering, even though it is suitable, you may not be able to reclaim all of your deposit. The purchase agreement should set out the terms under which a refund is available should matters not proceed to a satisfactory conclusion.

The franchise agreement

The franchise agreement proper is a much fuller and more detailed document. Broadly speaking, the process is divided into two phases. During the first phase, most of the onus is on the franchisor to help you set up your outlet.

The franchise agreement will lay down his obligation during this first stage to provide training, to help you raise finance, to help you find premises (or in the case of mobile franchise, a vehicle), obtain a lease, negotiate with the landlord, and perhaps to provide shopfitting, help with staff recruitment, and any other assistance that is agreed between the two parties. While that is going on, your role, which will of course be there in writing in the agreement, is to come up with the necessary money as and when it is needed, and to turn up for training and complete the course satisfactorily.

The second phase begins when you start trading. The part of the franchise agreement that covers this sets down in detail the contractual obligations of both parties (you will find that the franchisee has rather more to do during this phase than the franchisor – not surprising, really, as it is your business and you'll be running it), and covers matters such as fees, territory, advertising and termination of the contract.

The contract will begin by describing briefly the **nature of the franchise**, its trade marks, know-how, copyright and who owns them.

Next it will deal with the **length of the contract**. There are no hard and fast rules governing the duration of a franchise agreement but it is generally accepted that sufficient time should be allowed for the franchisee to recover his initial investment, and that is thought to be at least five years. At the end of that term there is usually an option to sign on for a further spell, maybe another five years, without paying an additional fee. (The exact details of the contract for the second term may be different in some respects from the first, because you will be expected to agree to the terms being offered to new franchisees at the time of your renewal, and they may not be quite the same as those to which you originally agreed.)

Territorial rights will be dealt with in detail. It is quite common for franchisors to offer exclusive rights to a territory. This should give the franchisee the incentive to exploit a promising potential market free from the competition of another franchisee belonging to the same organisation. (There is of course nothing to prevent franchisees from rival organisations competing with you in the same territory.)

Not all franchisors, however, are keen on allocating exclusive rights. They take the view that exclusivity carries with it the necessity to set performance targets lest a potentially promising territory may be wasted on a lazy franchisee. That in turn raises the problem of what to do if the performance targets are not met. This has the makings of a legal minefield into which no franchisor would willingly wish to tread. A compromise position is to grant exclusive rights for a limited period, so look at the franchise agreement carefully to see if such a restriction applies and if so under what circumstances the franchisor can reduce or change the territory.

Initial and continuing fees form an essential part of the contract. The agreement will set down how much you pay in initial fees and what you will get in return. You will probably pay these fees in instalments as and when materials and equipment are delivered, your training is undertaken, the premises are found, and so on. The timing of these payments should be stated plainly in the agreement, along with exactly what you are paying for at each stage. As with the deposit you paid when the purchase agreement was signed, there may be circumstances in which a whole or partial refund of the initial fee is available. If, for example, the franchisor decides that he has made a mistake and you are not after all a suitable franchisee (this could become apparent during the initial training period) you should be entitled to a full refund. If it is you who decides for any reason not to continue, you will almost certainly have to compensate the franchisor and will not therefore be entitled to recover all of your outlay.

The size and timing of the management services fees should be clearly stated in the agreement. So should the method by which they are to be calculated. The franchisor will want to make sure that he is not being diddled, so the agreement will contain provisions designed to protect his rights to obtain the full fees to which he is entitled. These may include conducting spot checks of the franchisee's books, stock levels, invoices and so on.

It is also usual for the franchisee to be required to conform to standard accountancy procedures so that the franchisor can make comparisons between the performance of different outlets and spot any anomalies that might suggest a franchisee is not declaring his full sales. The franchisor will probably insist on the franchisee producing profit and loss accounts at regular intervals and presenting audited statements of accounts annually.

If the franchisor receives his income not as a management fee but as a **mark-up** on goods sold to the franchisee, the agreement ought to declare the size of that mark-up and there ought also to be a clause governing the circumstances in which it can be increased.

The agreement will almost certainly make provision for an **advertising fund** (sometimes called a promotional fund) into which the franchisee must make regular payments. The terms and size of such payments should be clearly stated along with details of how the franchisor will spend the money, eg the proportion he will allocate to national advertising and the amount he will devote to promoting the franchisee's outlet.

Obligations

Now we come to the vital section of the agreement that sets down the dos and don'ts that govern the relationship between the franchisor and the franchisee. These will usually come under the headings 'obligations'.

Obligations of the franchisor

Typically these will contain items such as the following:

- **Training**. This section includes details such as when the training will take place, how long it will last and who pays for it (usually the franchisee).
- **Equipment**. A typical clause might be: 'The franchisor will arrange the supply of the initial equipment and advise and assist the franchisee in the requisition of all materials, stock and equipment necessary, the franchisee being liable and responsible for the cost of materials, stock and equipment.'
- **Decor**. In the case of retail franchises, the franchisor will provide designs and advice for the fitting and decoration of the shop and the installation of any equipment necessary. Any alterations to the decor will require the written approval of the franchisor.
- **Manuals**. The franchisor will issue to the franchisee a comprehensive and understandable operating manual. Ownership of manuals remains with the franchisor and no right of reproduction in any form is granted to the franchisee.
- **Advice and help**. The franchisor will provide continuing support and consultation concerning the conduct of the business throughout the term of the contract as the franchisor considers reasonable.

- **Records**. The franchisor will provide the franchisee with sales reports and accounts forms to assist the franchisee in maintaining accurate financial records.

Obligations of the franchisee

The obligations of the franchisee are, in the main, intended to protect the franchisor's reputation and goodwill and therefore lay down the standards that are expected of the franchisee. Here are a few typical items:

- **Conduct**. The franchisee must conduct himself and ensure that his employees conduct themselves in such a manner as not to discredit or denigrate the reputation of the business or its name. Any behaviour amounting, in the opinion of the franchisor, to misconduct if not properly abated shall be a cause for termination of the franchise.
- **Compliance**. The franchisee should use his best endeavours to comply with the systems and methods as set out in the operations manuals.
- **Premises**. To keep the premises in a good state of repair and internal decoration, and clean and tidy.
- **Staff standards**. To keep the outlet staffed with a sufficient number of competent employees so as to enable the outlet to operate efficiently to the highest standards prescribed by the franchisor, and if reasonably required by the franchisor, to arrange for staff to undergo training.
- **Goodwill**. Constantly to protect and promote the goodwill attached to the trade mark.
- **Access**. To permit the franchisor or his agents full, free and unrestricted access and right of entry to the outlet for any purpose whatsoever including, but not limited to, checking, ensuring or enforcing compliance by the franchisee with any of his obligations.

You will see from the above that the franchisee contract goes to some lengths to oblige the franchisee to play by the rules and stick to the systems. These demands should be reasonable and quite easily met by a conscientious franchisee. If, however, they strike you as particularly onerous or irksome – and bearing in mind that you cannot pick and choose those you wish to agree to – you might want to think again about what you are letting yourself in for and whether you can hack it.

Though both parties will set out with the good intention of seeing the contract through to its full term, there may be circumstances in which either wishes to terminate the agreement. These should be dealt with in the document.

Termination

Under **Termination by the Franchisor** you might expect to find clauses such as the following:

- The franchisor shall have the right in his absolute discretion to terminate the agreement for cause (which shall include but not be limited to a breach by the franchisee of any obligation covenant or duty contained herein) by giving written notice to the franchisee not less than 30 days prior to the date of termination and stating the reason for termination.
- If the notice of termination states that the cause for termination may be remedied then the franchisee shall have the right to remedy the same within 30 days and if all such causes are remedied to the satisfaction of the franchisor then he shall withdraw such notice.

The franchisor, therefore, can rid himself of a franchisee who breaks the rules or in some other way transgresses. This power should only be invoked if the franchisee is in serious breach of the agreement (cooking the books to avoid management services fees, for example) but your lawyer should be satisfied that the franchisor cannot terminate the agreement for some trivial breach of the rules.

Under **Termination by the Franchisee** the agreement may stipulate a period (say 36 months) from the starting date of the agreement after which the franchisee is free to terminate the contract. It will then set down the procedure to be followed, ie to give written notice and to surrender the lease (if any). It will also require the franchisee to pay any debts he owes to the franchisor (and to anyone else in connection with the business), to cease to represent himself as a franchisee, and to return stationery and other materials, including the operations manuals. As noted above, there will also be a requirement for the franchisee to surrender any leasehold interest and any fixtures or fittings. The franchisor will pay the franchisee the market value of these assets.

Sale or assignment clauses

Lastly, the franchise agreement will set out what happens if you want to sell the franchise or what will happen in the unfortunate circumstance of your death. You should have the right to sell the business to a third party (after all, one of the reasons for taking up a franchise is to build a business which grows in value and is a realisable asset should you want to retire or move on) but quite reasonably the franchisor will want a say in who you sell to.

The franchisee should have the right to assign his business to a third party ('assign' is a legal term meaning to transfer a property right to someone else), provided he complies with certain conditions laid down by the franchisor in the contract. These are usually to do with the franchisor making sure that anyone you sell to is a suitable person to take over and run the business. Expressed legally, that will probably be put in words such as 'a respectable and responsible person with the personal capacity and financial ability to perform the obligations of a franchisee under the franchise agreement. Furthermore, the prospective transferee shall at his own cost take and complete the training required of all new franchisees'.

It is quite common for agreements to give the franchisor the first right of refusal should the franchisee want to sell. There is nothing wrong with that. However, since the franchisee will want to be sure that he gets a fair price, the agreement should also set down the basis on which the business is to be valued. If the franchisor disposes of the business on behalf of the franchisee he will probably levy a charge for arranging the sale.

When you give up a franchise you are normally prevented under the terms of the agreement from starting a similar business in competition with the franchisor for a specified time after the sale (18 months is quite common). You are also prevented from disclosing any confidential information about the franchise, such as the contents of the operations manual, pricing policy or accounting systems, after the agreement is terminated.

Finally, on the death of a sole franchisee, his representatives will have a specified time, often six months from the date of the death, to inform the franchisor of their decision either to assign the business to any of the heirs of the franchisee or to a third party (in which case the franchisor must be satisfied that the new owners are suitable and fit people to run the business, and they for their part must go through the training programme) or to terminate the agreement and sell the business for its market value. On the death of a joint franchisee, it is usual for the surviving franchisee or franchisees to succeed in all respects to the rights of the deceased franchisee.

Now let us make haste from this morbid subject and turn to the life-enhancing task of preparing to meet the bank manager.

9
Raising the wind

Using a clearing bank

Few people relish the prospect of going along to a bank and asking to borrow money. Banks have a reputation for being stand-offish places for whom customers are not only a nuisance but in some indefinable way slightly suspect. Banks want you to trust them but are loath to return the compliment and trust you.

Whatever the truth of these impressions – and banks today insist they are warm, user-friendly institutions whose customers have nothing to fear – the good news is that as a prospective franchisee wanting to borrow money you are almost certain to get a far warmer welcome and meet with a great deal more encouragement than if you were an individual stepping in off the street with a business idea all of your own and a need to raise cash. Not for nothing have banks earned a reputation for being canny and cautious lenders who are as keen on security as a man who wears both belt and braces. They have, however, come to love franchising. Indeed, if the franchising industry were to want proof of its success it could find no more convincing an argument than the approval it has won from those ultra-cautious institutions – the banks.

Sometime in the 1970s they became aware that, unlike most business start-ups, which are a bad risk, new franchise outlets stand a reasonable chance of succeeding. The concept of combining the local knowledge, ambition and enthusiasm of an individual with the expertise and resources of a national, or even international, brand appealed to the belt-and-braces instinct in them.

In 1981, NatWest became the first of the big high street banks to set up a dedicated franchise section to gather information on the industry and to advise local managers who were being asked to lend to prospective franchisees. Today, the Bank of Scotland, HSBC, Lloyds, the Royal Bank of Scotland and NatWest all have departments specialising in franchising. Their job is to keep in touch with developments in franchising and to build files on individual franchise opportunities. So keen are some banks that they go one step further and actively promote franchising. HSBC, for example, sponsors the BFA's Franchisor and Franchisee of the Year Awards, and NatWest sponsors an annual survey of the industry. The upshot of all this knowledge and enthusiasm should be that when you walk into the local branch of your bank you will be met by a manager who, if he does not know about franchising himself, will certainly know a man or woman who does. In fact, you will almost certainly be invited to meet one of the bank's team of local business managers to discuss your project further. No bank will go so far as to recommend a particular franchise – that would expose them to the risk of legal liability should things subsequently go wrong and the franchise outlet fail – but they will offer guidance and advice.

It is a measure of the banks' enthusiasm for franchising that not only will they give you a more favourable hearing than if you were any old business start-up, they will also lend to you on more favourable terms. An independent start-up can expect to borrow no more than 50 per cent of the total cost of setting up the business. By contrast a new franchisee with an established franchise will be able to borrow as much as 70 per cent. (It's a bit different if the franchise is new and relatively untried, in which case the bank may not go higher than 50 per cent.) Not only that, the chances are you won't pay as much interest as an independent start-up and you may need to offer less security for loans.

If you followed the advice earlier in this book you should have a good idea how much of your own money you can afford to invest, which will, in turn, have determined your choice of franchise. Now you must set about persuading the bank to lend you the remaining 70 per cent of the start-up costs (assuming, of course, that your savings come to 30 per cent of those costs – you might be able to put in more than 30 per cent. Much will depend not only on how much you can afford to invest in the business but also on whether you really want to sink your entire savings into the venture).

Incidentally, if you are wondering why the bank won't lend more than 70 per cent, the answer is that the payment of interest will come out of the cashflow of your business and larger loans could prove an impossibly onerous burden.

Franchise finance packages

A business requires two types of capital. Fixed capital is the money you put in to buy the business and set it up. It covers items such as premises, equipment and legal fees. Working capital is what you need to keep the business going while you are waiting for money to come in. The usual arrangement is to arrange a 'term loan'(ie a loan for a fixed amount with a fixed repayment schedule) for the fixed capital, and an overdraft to cover the working capital.

An overdraft is a flexible form of borrowing, which has the advantage that you pay only for the funds you use. The bank will arrange a combination of the two to suit your requirements. Better still, it will, in many cases, have a ready-made franchise package developed in cooperation with the franchisor. This will apply in those cases where the bank has experience of, and confidence in, the franchise organisation you are about to become part of. Finance packages have a number of advantages: they tend to speed up the lending process; they may include more favourable terms than you would get if you were buying a franchise less well-known to the bank; and, from the franchisor's point of view, they give promising recruits a smoother ride over the bumpy road to obtaining funding.

The Small Firms Loan Guarantee Scheme

Now, having said how keen the banks are to lend to new franchisees, I may have given the impression that it's all a bit of breeze. If so, it's time to correct that. Bankers like franchising, but they also like prudence, and that means running checks over everything including – indeed, starting with – you. Before lending you the money, the bank will want to know about your background, qualifications, training, financial resources and suitability to run the business. It helps that the franchisor will also have wanted to satisfy himself on those points and will be able to pass on his findings to the bank.

The bank will also want to know as much as possible about the outlet you are planning to open – what will be its prospects in the locality you have chosen? Where are the loan repayments coming from? What level of sales are needed to break even? What assumptions have been made about cashflow? And after assessing the risk of lending to you, the bank may ask for security against the loan – a life policy possibly, or the value of your home minus any outstanding mortgage debt.

If no security is available you may be able to take advantage of the Government's Small Business Service (SBS) Small Firms Loan Guarantee Scheme. This guarantees loans from the banks and other financial institutions for small firms that have viable business proposals but who have tried and failed to get a conventional loan because of a lack of security. Loans are available for periods of between two and ten years, in sums from £5,000 to £100,000. SBS guarantees 70 per cent of the loan. In return for the guarantee, the borrower pays SBS a premium of 1.5 per cent a year on the outstanding amount of the loan. The premium is reduced to 0.5 per cent if the loan is taken at a fixed rate of interest. The commercial aspects of the loan are matters between the borrower and the lender. The bank will advise you about how to apply for a loan guarantee, and, because the loan is guaranteed by the government and therefore represents a low credit risk to the bank, you are likely to get very favourable interest rates.

I know this all sounds rather daunting, but as a prospective franchisee you have the inestimable advantage of a friend and ally in the shape of the franchisor. He is used to dealing with banks. He knows the questions they will ask and he can help you to prepare the answers. And the bank is reassured by the fact that the franchisor shares its desire for you to succeed: no franchisor wants a failure and the bank can take comfort in the knowledge that the franchisor will be monitoring your progress and helping you along.

How to prepare a business plan

Whether or not the bank finally comes up with the loan you ask for is a decision entirely in the hands of the bank's local, or sometimes regional, business manager[1] (NatWest has a team of over 100 specialist Area Franchise Managers who deal with loan applications). That is because the bank takes the view that its staff out in the country, rather than at head office, are best placed to make a judgment about local trading conditions and to weigh up your character and prospects. After all, it is you who wants the loan and will be running the business.

It follows that it is vital to present a good case to the bank manager. Although the bank's franchise department will have supplied him with up-to-date information about the franchise in which you want to invest, he will still want to know the details of your proposed outlet. That means you must draw up a business plan. This is your chance to impress. Nothing pleases a bank manager more than a thoroughly thought out and clearly presented business plan. It makes his day. The very fact of drawing up the plan will help you too.

The business plan is exactly that – a plan. A plan of attack, if you like. It sets out in simple terms the nature of the business, the market you intend to conquer, the weapons at your disposal, the reasons why you will succeed, and the gains you expect to make. Following the process

---

1. So for 'bank manager' in what follows, read 'business manager'.

through in your mind and setting it all down, step by step, on paper, will give you the clearest indication yet of what lies ahead of you: the challenge, the tactics, the goals.

The usefulness of the plan does not end when the business manager rises from his chair, shakes you by the hand, smiles warmly, and gives you the money. It stays with you as a continuing chart to guide your business and monitor its progress. It enables you to compare your actual performance with your forecast performance, allowing you either to congratulate yourself on your achievements or work out what's gone wrong and how it can be put right before it gets out of hand.

It is important that the business plan strikes the right balance between optimism and realism. You must never lose sight of the fact that the plan is, above all, an advertisement for yourself and your project: when it is put before the bank manager its whole aim is to advance your case in a persuasive, and if at all possible, exciting way, giving detailed reasons why you will succeed and therefore why the bank will get its money back. Even so, there is a narrow dividing line between skilful promotion and overselling. The aim should be to state your case convincingly and realistically, not to promise the moon.

As we have noted earlier, bank managers are by nature cautious – they have to be: it's not their money they are lending, it's the bank's – and they feel far more comfortable with projections that sound achievable rather than surprising. (That doesn't mean that you shouldn't set out to surprise yourself. Some business start-ups have two business plans – one for the bank manager that errs on the side of conservatism, another for themselves that sets higher – though nevertheless attainable – targets and acts as a spur.)

This book has emphasised throughout the advantages that you, as a prospective franchisee, have over those poor souls who set out to start a business all on their own. Unlike them, you have a guide, a mentor, a counsellor, someone who's been there before, knows the ropes, and is backing you all the way. And never will you have been more grateful for that experience than when it comes to drawing up the business plan. You may not be used to organising your thoughts in writing; it is unlikely that you will have prepared profit and cashflow forecasts before; you may well be nervous about making a presentation to the bank. The franchisor is there to help with all of those things. He knows how to make your business plan look professional and how best to put your case. That said, the more you do yourself, the firmer will be your grasp of the proposition and the more confident and convincing will be your presentation.

There is no such thing as a standard plan. They vary from individual to individual and from location to location. But all have a number of features in common. Typically, the headings and contents are as follows.

The business

The nature of the product or service; its history and its unique selling proposition (if any). With an established franchise the bank manager will know about these things so they need not be set out in great detail. A newer franchise will require greater explanation. Just as important – perhaps more important – than the background of the business are the qualities that you will be bringing to it. The bank manager will want to know why you are keen to run your own business, your ambitions, your targets.

The market

Arguably the single most important part of the plan. Unless there are sufficient customers waiting out there for your product or service – or at any rate waiting to be persuaded to buy – you will be finished before you start. This section should include:

- the likely size of the market;
- the type of customers you will be targeting, eg businesses or private individuals;
- who you will be competing with and why you are likely to do better than them.

Marketing

Here you outline the ways in which you plan to attract customers. Will the franchisor be supporting you with national advertising? How will you be promoting the product or service locally? How do you propose to measure the results?

The people

The bank manager will want to know about you and any staff you are taking on. What experience do you have? What qualifications? Of course, as a franchisee, it is quite likely that you will have no previous experience in the particular field in which you plan to operate, or indeed no experience of running a business at all. Nevertheless your background may be helpful. You may be able to show that you have organisational skills, for instance. And with any franchise it helps to have an outgoing, confident personality regardless of previous employment. If you come across as a good 'people person', that will help to persuade the bank manager that you can promote your own business.

Of course, a great strength of franchising is the ability of the franchisor to take an army sergeant, a housewife and a software programmer and turn them into a fast food restaurateur, a mortgage broker and a publican. So this part of your plan should give details of the training that you and your staff (if any) are going to receive.

Sales

Related to, but not the same as, marketing. This section covers items such as the price you intend to charge and how it compares with the competition; the profit margin on sales; the source of supplies (will you be tied to the franchisor or will you be free to look elsewhere?); and the credit facilities you might receive from suppliers.

Premises and equipment

The bank manager will be interested in your premises for a number of reasons. He will want to satisfy himself that they are in a suitable location and he will want to know how much you need to spend on fitting them out. You will need to include details such as whether the property is leasehold or freehold, the terms and costs involved, rates, and rent reviews. As for equipment, you will need to list what you need, where you will be getting it from, its cost, and whether you will be leasing or buying. The more help you are getting from the franchisor in finding premises and obtaining equipment, the more reassured the bank manager will be.

Finance

This is the part that most concerns the bank manager. It sets out your assets (eg the value of your home less mortgage, your savings, insurance and other assets) and states your financial requirements. Using the franchisor's experience and knowledge you will need to prepare a projected profit and loss account and a cashflow forecast. The detailed information in these two forecasts will form the basis of your case for raising finance and will show how much you are likely to need to cover working capital in the form of an overdraft and how much you will need to borrow in the form of a term loan to help cover the costs of setting up the business.

Start with a brief **summary** of the facts: the forecast profit (or loss)[2] for the first year and the likely 'break-even point' for the business. This term needs explanation: the break-even point is the point at which your sales are large enough to cover your overheads. So first you need to tot up all your overheads (also known as fixed costs) – rent, rates, insurance, telephone, stationery, postage, and the actual costs of starting the business such as premises, equipment and stock. Once you know that figure you can work out how many sales you will need to cover those overheads. Break through the break-even barrier and you are into profit – the whole point of being in business and the measure of your success.

---

2. Don't panic. It's not uncommon for a new business to budget for a loss while it gets established.

Next you will need to state how the costs are to be covered, ie how much of your own money you are putting in and how much you will need from the bank. It's important in making these calculations to take into account the fact that you and your family are going to need to eat – so work out your 'income', the money you are going to need to take out of the business to cover everyday living expenses.

Next comes the **profit and loss forecast**. This is a statement of your predicted sales minus your direct costs (all costs directly related to your products or service such as materials; another way of looking at this is to see them as the costs incurred in making the sales) and overheads (wages, rent rates, telephone etc).

The **cashflow forecast** will probably be different from the profit and loss forecast, for the good reason that profit and cash are not the same thing. It is a cliché that cash is the lifeblood of a business, but like most clichés it's true all the same. One of the biggest reasons for business failure is that the flow of money going out exceeds the trickle of money coming in. This can happen for a number of reasons, but the most common cause is, quite simply, slow payers. Small businesses who supply large companies often find to their cost that the bigger the organisation the worse it is at paying up.

Fortunately, since franchises tend to sell either to the general public or to other small businesses, few find themselves at the mercy of large companies. (It's worth mentioning at this point that franchises that enjoy a good cashflow, such as those where the customer hands over the money for goods or services immediately on delivery, quite understandably, use this as a strong selling point when recruiting new franchisees. Worries over cashflow are a potential headache that every new business could do without.)

Even so, seasonal factors can affect cashflow so it's common sense to plan for an uneven flow of money into the business. You are in trouble the moment that bills have to be paid faster than cash is coming in. Many small businesses have found to their cost that it's no good knowing that a big order will bring in a big profit if you cannot afford to pay for the labour or materials needed to complete the order. Cashflow must always be under control, which is why a cashflow forecast is essential. Once you have the figures down on paper they will help you to anticipate when you might not have enough cash; they will show you when you might have some extra cash that you could make use of; and they will help you to make more efficient use of your resources.

A cashflow forecast is a record of when you expect to receive money into your business and when you expect to pay it out. Since it is a moving picture of money that we are talking about rather than a snapshot, you look at it over a period of time, usually monthly and for at least one year ahead. The aim of the game is to show the bank manager when your need for cash might be at its greatest and therefore the likely size and pattern of your funding needs. The bank will give you a blank cashflow form to fill in and the good old franchisor will help you to do it. Where would you be without him?

The details will vary according to the nature of the business, but broadly speaking the headings will be **opening balance** (how much is in your account at the start of each month, or how much it is overdrawn), **total receipts** (cash from sales, cash from debtors), **total payments** (eg payment to suppliers, cash purchases, rent, heating, lighting, telephones, bank interest etc). If receipts exceed payments in any one month that is called a net inflow. If payments exceed receipts that's called – guess what? – a net outflow. The **closing balance** (the balance brought forward from the previous month added to total receipts and minus total payments) then becomes the opening balance at the start of the next month. It sounds complicated but once you've worked it out a few times and seen it down on paper it's not that tricky. Believe me.

And that just about wraps it up as far as preparing the forecasts are concerned. Now you must steel yourself for the dreaded interview.

Approaching your bank

Actually it's not as bad as that, provided you prepare thoroughly. Treat it as though you were an actor playing a part. I don't mean you have to make things up or pretend to be something you're not. Still less that you should think of your presentation as a piece of fiction. That would be disastrous. What I mean is that you should rehearse your application. Practise in front of a mirror. Get a relative or friend to play the part of the bank manager and lead him or her through your presentation. The two words you must have at the back of your mind are conviction and enthusiasm. You must show that you know your stuff and truly believe in it. The more convinced you are, the more convincing you will be.

If you have prepared your business plan thoroughly you should have all the facts at your fingertips. Earlier in this chapter we covered the main headings – the business, the market, the people and so on. What you have to do is talk the bank manager through the plan – elaborating where you think fit and quite possibly fielding some awkward questions along the way. Don't take it amiss if the bank manager affects a sceptical approach. Lending money is a serious business and he will want to satisfy himself that you have done your homework. In all probability he will already have been briefed on the franchise operation in which you are planning to invest. Even so, he will want to hear you explain it in your own words. What he is looking for is not just a grasp of the basic figures (though you should of course have that) but also that you have an awareness of the risk you are taking – as we have seen, no business is without risk and that is true of franchising – and that you are motivated, enthusiastic, and, above all, really keen to work for yourself.

Presentation tips

Here are a few more tips about the presentation. Obvious perhaps, but it does no harm to spell them out.

- **Look your best**. Even in a trendy, dress-down world, bank managers are sober citizens. They have to be. Money is no laughing matter and has to be approached with a sombre reverence. It is, therefore, a good idea to dress conventionally when you are in the presence of a custodian of the coffers.

- Be sure that **your business plan looks neat and smart**, too. It should be well printed, laid out without too much clutter or detail, and not too long, perhaps no more than 20 pages.
- In making your presentation have five or six **key points** in mind. These should be the things you find most exciting and promising about the venture, the reasons why you are confident of success.
- **The money**. You must be absolutely clear about how much you want to borrow, in what form (overdraft and/or loan), and why.

And that ought to be that. Once the loan is agreed, you can sign the franchise agreement and set about the exciting task of getting your fledgling business up and flying.

10
The ups, downs, and ups again

Your franchise relationship

So what happens next? Well, in the best of all possible worlds you will go on to enjoy a rewarding and fulfilling life as a self-employed business person. If you have researched and planned in the way outlined in this book you will certainly be well-placed to succeed. You will have a tried and tested system, the encouragement and support of an experienced franchisor, and the backing of a bank with a vested interest in your success. It would, however, be foolish to imagine that your franchising adventure will be plain sailing. Every business has its ups and downs, every entrepreneur, even of the 'lite' variety, has black moments. Franchising is no different.

Earlier we likened the relationship between franchisee and franchisor to a marriage, and it's remarkable how close the parallels are. At first the married couple set off happily united. Only later do they discover irritating defects in each other. One leaves hairs in the washbasin, the other squeezes the toothpaste in the middle of the tube. The stresses and strains of being together are telling. There are arguments, sometimes heated. But, with luck and time, compromises are reached, tacit understandings made, and the two rub along, each more or less content with the other, neither wanting to spoil the hard won achievements of being together.

A wealth of evidence, some anecdotal, some researched,[1] shows that most franchise relationships change and develop over time in a fairly

---

1. According to the BFA/NatWest survey dislikes were mentioned by 84 per cent of franchisees, including the following: paying ongoing fees – 18 per cent; franchisor can change the rules – 12 per cent; long working hours – 12 per cent; having to adhere to franchise system – 10 per cent.

predictable way. At first there is the honeymoon period. During the initial training the franchisee learns a lot quickly. It is a rewarding and exciting time, with the franchisor giving and the franchisee gratefully receiving. This peaceful coexistence continues during the early months of the business; the franchisee is still learning, the franchisor is on hand to help. But then comes the tricky period. The franchisee becomes familiar with the systems and grows in confidence. The business really feels as though it belongs to him (which it does) and as if it was all his own work (which it wasn't). Worse, he begins to resent the continuing presence in the background – and sometimes in the foreground – of the franchisor. What was once help begins to look uncommonly like interference. And as if that wasn't bad enough, the franchisor is forever creaming money off the top in the shape of management services fees. It's as bad as taxation; you earn the money through your own labours and someone else comes along with his hand out and takes a cut. Not only that, the franchisee begins to have his own ideas about how the business should be run, how it can be improved. And yet there he is stuck with rigid rules and systems, unable to deviate from the path laid down.

When things reach a really low point it's not uncommon for a franchisee to seek an early termination of the contract. Far better, of course, if this dissatisfaction is a passing phase and the franchisee comes, on reflection, to appreciate that continuing control by the franchisor serves to maintain standards throughout the network and is in everyone's interest. Ideally, then, the relationship settles down and proves mutually satisfying and profitable.

Minimising friction

Knowing that friction can arise – indeed, is almost inevitable – what can be done to minimise it? First, it pays to pick the right partner at the outset. As we have seen, the best kind of franchisee is someone who is prepared to take some risk but appreciates the greater security offered by franchising compared to going it alone; someone who is neither a strong team player nor a loner but would be happy with the middle ground of being part of a franchised network; above all, someone who would relish the independence and self-esteem of being his or her own boss.

The ideal franchisor

The ideal franchisor is mature, experienced, considerate and tactful. He is leader, diplomat and creative thinker. He is, in short, a paragon, and probably as difficult to find as the ideal franchisee. Even so, the closer one can get to matching the most desirable characteristics on both sides the better, which means bringing together people who long to be their own boss with established franchisors who know their stuff.

It follows that the greatest difficulty occurs when a company is new to franchising. An inexperienced franchisor will be in a hurry to recruit and is therefore likely to make mistakes. The hurry comes from the pressures faced by a new franchise company that is itself a small business. As Professor Stanworth of the University of Westminster points out, a new franchise has to construct a front-end infrastructure of managerial support some years ahead of achieving full financial break-even point: 'Given the demands placed upon an infant franchise system to finance and manage the processes of franchisee recruitment and all that entails, plus induction and field support for franchisees, the new franchise company is, in effect, developing the management and administrative structure normally associated with a medium-sized business, without the income levels normally associated with this scale of business. For a small business intent on developing into a credible franchise operation, the strains normally associated with small business growth are, in fact, likely to be magnified and concentrated, rather then reduced.'

So you can see why recruitment is not always shrewd and carefully planned: the franchisor is so keen to make his first sale that he is perhaps not as selective as he ought to be. The risk is not necessarily that the franchisee will be lazy or inefficient; rather that he may turn out to be an independent spirit who will become dissatisfied with the franchise relationship and, worse still, turn into a trouble-maker who spreads dissatisfaction throughout the network.

Incidentally, there is another problem that can arise from a new franchise company's early recruitment. At first, when there are just a handful of new franchisees, they will naturally be close to the franchisor. They may be in contact daily, almost certainly they will be on first-name terms. But as the franchise grows and prospers and the network expands, those first franchisees may begin to feel neglected, that they are just cogs on the wheel. That early sense of chumminess and belonging may turn into dissatisfaction and chippiness.

Maintaining morale

This is where the skilful franchisor comes into his own. He will constantly be looking for ways to maintain morale and build a team spirit. One way to hold the interest of franchisees and to continue to reap the benefits of their energy and enterprise is to encourage them to take on a second franchise. Their earlier success is rewarded, they face a new challenge, their financial prospects are enhanced, and their self-esteem is boosted. Some franchises achieve a similar effect by encouraging franchisees to start from small beginnings – perhaps working from home and doing the 'job' themselves, it could be anything from valeting cars to cleaning carpets – and then, as the business becomes established, to move into an office, recruit staff, and take on a more managerial role. Another way to build and maintain team spirit is to hold regular get-togethers, allowing the whole franchise network to socialise, exchange views and have fun. Some companies use these occasions to reward outstanding performance, perhaps by choosing a Franchisee of the Year and paying for them to go on a foreign holiday.

Because some elements of conflict are inevitable in the franchise relationship – they may even be beneficial in the way that creative tension is beneficial, provided they don't get out of hand – a wise franchisor will allow some mechanism for the expression of the views of franchisees. He may, for instance, set up a consultative committee or encourage the formation of a franchisee association, or both. The key is to have an open-door policy and to avoid at all costs the building up of an us-and-them mentality.

A good franchisor will communicate regularly with franchisees using occasional reports and a regular newsletter. He will sort out their problems, real or imaginary, and he will be available and approachable. When disputes arise it's often down to poor communication, with franchisees thinking the franchisor is arrogant, busy or simply not interested, and the franchisor suspecting that a dissatisfied franchisee is nagging, incompetent or simply not committed. With care, all that can be avoided. Neither party should lose sight of the fact that franchising is a partnership, a two-way relationship in which both sides need each other. As one franchisor is fond of saying, 'We never lose sight of the fact that our success depends on the franchisees' success.'

Individual enterprise

I'd like to conclude this chapter by mentioning, almost as an extended footnote, that some franchise relationships are less rigid than others. It's never wise to generalise, and earlier I have stressed that franchises do not as a rule allow much scope for individual enterprise or initiative; they much prefer, in the interests of maintaining standards and uniformity, that franchisees stick pretty closely to the laid down formula.

There are, however, exceptions to every rule, as several finalists for a recent BFA Franchisee of the Year award prove. The theme for the competition was 'Adding Value' and it showed that some franchisors are keen to encourage franchisees to come up with ideas of their own.

For instance, Wenda Williams runs a Stagecoach Theatre school in Derby. The franchisor started out by offering singing, dance and drama classes for six to 16-year-olds, an idea that proved so successful that today there are more than 400 schools in the UK and others in Ireland, Malta, the USA, Spain, Gibraltar, Germany and Australia. However, when Wenda found that parents would bring along younger siblings who were keen to join in, she had the idea of introducing Early Stages – classes for four to six-year-olds. She put her idea to Stagecoach and piloted the scheme in Derby. It has since been adopted by the entire franchise network and generates an income of nearly £1.8 million a year.

Stewart Maze operates a Snap-on Tools franchise in South Antrim, selling tools and equipment to garage mechanics from a mobile showroom. Seeing his customers excitedly gazing at his stock it occurred to him that they could be 'just like big kids'. So he started giving them lollipops. His secret marketing tool – a fruit flavoured lollipop – proved so successful it was taken up by Snap-on throughout its 390-strong network and the franchise now hands out lollies bearing the company's logo.

Husband-and-wife business partners Kevin and Gaynor Surgett run a Durham Pine furniture franchise in Ipswich. Unusually for a franchise company, Durham allowed the couple to launch their own advertising and promotional campaign. The results were spectacular. In two years they doubled their turnover from £500,000 to £1 million pounds. The strategy was so successful that other Durham Pine stores throughout the UK have copied it.

In each case the franchisee's imagination and initiative was welcomed by the franchisor and the entire network benefited. There could scarcely be better examples of good franchising practice in action.

11
It's a woman thing

By now the perceptive reader will have noticed the trouble I have had with the third person pronoun. Sometimes I have written 'he', other times the more clumsy 'he or she'. I have also assumed for ease of expression that all franchisors (and all bank managers for that matter) are male. Now is the time to apologise for these solecisms and set matters straight. Franchising is not, and never has been, a man's world. If there are more men than women in franchising that is no more than a reflection of the fact that there are more men than women running small businesses in general. But that picture is changing and franchising can pride itself in being in the vanguard.

Women are already a formidable force in franchising. They head a significant number of franchise operations; they account for around a quarter of all franchisees in the UK; and they are making their mark as professional franchise specialists in banking, consulting and the law. Moreover some franchise companies are specifically targeting women in their recruitment campaigns.

Suits you, madam

There are a number of reasons for the growing numbers of women in the franchise world. The first and most obvious is that a desire to be your own boss is not a uniquely male thing. In fact, given that too many women still find it hard to get the recognition and promotion they feel they deserve, it could be argued that the impetus to 'go it alone' is greater for women than for men.

The beauty of franchising, however, is that you don't go it alone in isolation; the very way it is structured, with ready-made systems, training and continuing support, might have been designed with women in mind, since everything about it is designed to build confidence and bring out the innate skills of the franchisee.

It would be foolish to deny that there are differences between the attitudes and aptitudes of men and women. At the risk of generalising – and there really is no other way of making the point – men tend to be more stubborn than women, more convinced that there are circumstances in which it might be necessary to reinvent the wheel, and moreover that they are the very people to do it. Women, on the other hand, tend to be good listeners, good at building relationships, willing to pay attention to detail, and able to establish priorities. Men, of course, can do those things too, but experience suggests that these attributes occur more consistently and reliably in women. This again makes for a good relationship between females and franchising. To generalise again, most women, unlike most men, are happy to follow tried and tested systems, to stick to the established formula, to accept that the franchisor has been there before and knows what she is talking about. (I'm trying to cure that pronoun problem.)

A third reason why franchising suits women and vice versa is its flexibility. Many women want businesses they can run from home and fit in around a young family. There are a growing number of franchises that allow them to do that. Indeed, some franchises were started by women for women.

Success stories

For instance, desperate to find ways to amuse her pre-school children, Gill Thomas drew on her business experience and musical background to start a series of classes under the name Musical Minors. That was in 1991. The classes were so successful that four years later she launched the business as a national franchise, changing its name to Jo Jingles. At the last count there were more than 50 franchisees running music classes for children in over 300 locations throughout the UK.

Dorset-based Formative Fun was set up in 1991 by Jane Warren, a former teacher and a mother of two, to sell educational toys and games. Today there are retail outlets, a nationwide network of distributors, a thriving mail order service and a Web site.

Flowers Forever is Britain's only wedding bouquet preservation franchise. Its managing director, Moya Hammond, says women have the skills to manage and grow a small business, but some lack the confidence to try. She has helped many to overcome their initial doubts and build thriving businesses. 'Some of our most successful franchisees have started their businesses with very low self confidence,' she says. 'And they have surprised themselves. Women do not always recognise their own capabilities – particularly if they have taken a career break lasting several years. For such people franchising is ideal. It can provide the support necessary to enable the individual to develop her skills within a safe environment.'

Pam Bader, Chief Executive of the domestic cleaning franchise Molly Maid, says: 'When it comes to success, the franchisee's gender is not an issue'. She concedes, however, that women generally fit well into a maid service franchise. She cites the 'softer skills' needed to win the trust and confidence of people who naturally take great care before handing over the keys to their homes. Currently over 60 per cent of Molly Maid franchisees are women. They tend to be drawn from managerial backgrounds. Sherry Costello, for example, was a senior administrator for a large municipal organisation before setting off on her own. 'My main reason for starting the franchise was to show that I could run a business and a family side-by-side, and be financially independent,' she says. 'My father, who has owned many businesses, was against me doing this franchise, but after seeing my determination and commitment, and the growth of the business, he is now fully behind me, offering not only his support but his knowledge too. I only hope that I can continue to make him proud of me, as I know he already is.'

She says she wanted to run her own business, but didn't feel confident enough to 'go it alone'. 'Franchising offered me the chance to be my own boss, but with the back-up of the franchisor behind me.' She finds staffing the hardest part of the business. 'The old saying, "you're only as good as your staff", is so true. They let you down, they have little or no commitment, which is very frustrating. But I now have several very good members of staff and that helps me to sleep at night.' Her advice to prospective franchisees is, 'Research your subject very well. Listen to other franchisees. Contact the BFA and check out the prospective franchisor. Have the full backing of your family. Be determined to succeed.'

There are countless other examples of successful women franchisees, and by no means all are in what might be called 'traditional women's areas' such as fashion, health and beauty (though plenty are). Alexis DeJean runs a Jani-King contract cleaning business in East Anglia. Within a year of taking up her franchise, she tripled her original business target and hit a turnover of £200,000. She then set her sights on £1 million.

A single mother with two young children, she worked in the airline business in the USA before returning to the UK to run a rental and clothing business. Soon, however, she was looking for a franchise. 'I decided to go into franchising because I wanted something that would put me into an upper bracket,' she says. 'I wanted that corporate image. I wanted to run my own business but with the support of a large company behind me. I looked at a number of options but what attracted me to Jani-King was its professionalism. It's a young, vibrant, upwardly mobile company that's expanding and has the edge on its competitors.' Her clients include large companies such as Luminar and Scottish & Newcastle, and she employs a staff of between 50 and 60 people. 'I love my business, I can't get enough of it,' she says. 'You need to have organisational skills, and you need to have a liking for people because our whole time is spent dealing with people. You also need to keep a professional edge about you because Jani-King is the McDonald's of the cleaning world. You're not just a Mrs

Mop, you are a professional who's going to do a job to the best of your ability.'

Margaret Taylor found she had time on her hands after taking early retirement from a career in nursing and wanted to run a business. Bravely, she picked a sector in which she had no previous experience, but within a few months she was on target to turnover £1 million in her first year. She runs a Global Travel agency near Wrexham and chose the business because 'travel is an exciting and enjoyable sector'. 'Global interested me because of its membership framework and the expertise and support it offered. When I first decided to sign on I didn't know anything about travel, but because the training was first-rate that wasn't a problem.'

Partnerships

All these success stories and more prove that franchising is especially well suited to women of all ages and from a variety of backgrounds. It is, however, an argument that can be taken too far. In truth, a great many franchisees, women and men, run their business with the support, and often the help, of their spouses or partners.

Fergus and Clair Belcher run an Urban Planters franchise in Reading supplying and looking after indoor plants in offices, hotels and shopping centres. The former National Farmers Union Secretary and his wife took on the business because they wanted to work together after the birth of their first child. They did so well they were awarded a prize for achieving the best quality of plant care throughout the national franchise network.

John and Sue Price from Mytholmroyd near Halifax are also prizewinners. The couple are franchisees with Stainbusters, a national carpet and soft-furnishing cleaning specialists, and they have twice walked off with the company's Franchisee of the Year award. John took on the franchise in 1997 after 23 years as a production supervisor. Sue joined him as the business developed. 'The great thing about Stainbusters is the system is so clearly laid down in the manuals,' he says. 'We also receive great support from head office, and the team spirit throughout the network is second to none.'

Jill D'Crus went into business with her son Greg. She had extensive administrative experience and he was keen on cars. Together they investigated the possibilities and discovered Fleet Mobile Tyres. The Cambridge-based company supplies and fits tyres to company cars in the business-to-business sector, and to private motorists through its online division ETyres. It says it has plenty of examples of successful husband-and-wife joint ventures, and several father-and-son partnerships, but Jill and Greg, who run their business in Plymouth, are the first mother-and-son partnership.

The last word

I leave the last word to someone who speaks with authority about women and franchising. Cathryn Hayes is National Franchise Manager at HSBC and the first woman to hold such a position in UK banking. She says franchising's wide range of industry sectors, investment levels and methods of doing business offers women the flexibility to match their business to their family commitments, a consideration that continues to affect them much more than it does men. 'Many women who have been running a home and raising a family have many of the attributes needed to run a business successfully – they are decisive, energetic, organise well and are used to doing at least three things at once. If you have these qualities you may be well suited to running your own business, but if you are unsure what to do then franchising could be just the thing.'

Case studies

Domino's Pizza

Founded in 1960, Domino's Pizza is one of the most successful franchised networks in the world. The company has over 7,000 stores in more than 50 markets and employs around a quarter of a million team members. Domino's opened its first UK store in Luton in 1985 and its first Irish store in Dublin in 1991, and has since grown to deliver around 10 million pizzas a year. The company has around 320 stores and 120 franchisees in the UK and Ireland.

Jeff Reid is one of Domino's newest franchisees but he illustrates the appeal of the business. After a decade of selling cars to American military personnel throughout Europe, he thought it was time to consider a change of career.

'I was keen to relocate my family to the UK and I wanted to be self-employed and enjoy more of the fruits of my labour,' he says. 'It was at this point that a friend suggested franchising. As I did my research, I saw that Domino's franchisees were seeing excellent returns on investment – about 15 of them own businesses that are worth more than £1 million each. The Domino's franchise offered me both the safety of an established brand and substantial opportunities for expansion.'

The home-delivered food market is going from strength to strength. In 2002 it was valued at £1.058 billion, a 56 per cent rise since 1997. According to Mintel's research into Evening Eating Habits (September 2003), it is set to keep expanding. The report said that the 'out-of-home eating experience' is increasingly being replicated in the home, a development that Domino's is well placed to take advantage of.

Jeff Reid opened his first Domino's Pizza store in Crewe in December 2003. He says, 'The pizza delivery market was booming and there were opportunities with Domino's to build my own "pizza delivery empire",

Jeff Reid

particularly in the North West. I knew that the company readily encourages franchisees to own multiple units and is committed to supporting its franchisees as they expand. My aim is to have a cluster of stores by 2006.'

Before making the commitment to join a franchise, he wanted to be convinced by every part of the offer – the franchisor's support and training, the brand, image and of course, the product. He says:

> Customers know what to expect with a Domino's pizza and I have to admit, I'm a big fan. On my own, I would never be able to find the quality, fresh pizza ingredients at the price that Domino's is able to negotiate. Three times a week, it delivers fresh dough to the store – you can really taste the difference, and without the company delivering it, I'd have to spend my nights mixing it up. Also, as part of the franchise agreement, I have the Domino's image: the modern store fascia, the clearly identifiable uniform and the packaging. This gives me a clear advantage over local independents who could never enjoy the same quality of design and the same strength of image.

The modern store fascia

Strong brand awareness gives me a real head start over local independents. The national advertising fund, which receives regular contributions from every franchisee, has enabled Domino's to finance national advertising, a marketing programme that includes the distribution of 120 million menus a year and the highly successful sponsorship of *The Simpsons* on Sky One. The company has established itself ahead of all its competitors on every major interactive TV channel and also on the Internet. It has cornered the online food delivery market and automatically provided me with extra sales channels.

He says the first couple of weeks as a franchisee were quite a shock to the system:

I lost nearly three stone in weight whilst launching the store. There was so much to do – I needed to recruit and train team members, establish certain systems for keeping the store running smoothly

Make-line and Domino's packaging

and attract and serve customers. Luckily, Domino's had prepared me by sending me to the launch of a new store in Coalville, Leicestershire as a dress rehearsal six months earlier. I am certain the first month at my own store would have been a lot harder if I hadn't already been through it once already.

Six months later, he has no regrets. 'I am so glad I took the plunge. At last I am getting the chance to run my own business and I think it's going to be a great success.'

Domino's is a fully accredited member of the British Franchise Association and is a franchising success story spanning over 40 years. The company believes the key to its success is the dedication of its franchisees and the company's emphasis on quality ingredients, service and image.

Taking on a Domino's franchise is a sound business opportunity for the right sort of person, as franchisees receive the backing of a trusted, successful brand and proven business model. It requires a considerable investment in terms of time and money but the rewards can be significant.

Case study: Domino's Pizza / 123

How to find out more

Domino's aims to recruit the highest quality franchisees – businessmen and women who will demonstrate commitment to the brand and deliver the best product and customer service in the pizza delivery industry. The typical initial start-up cost for a store is £210,000 (exclusive of VAT). Of this at least £80,000 must be in ready cash.

Applications are rigorously reviewed by Domino's franchise sales team who look for strong evidence of the candidate's competency in managing people and finances. Extensive training is given to all new franchisees, who must spend time working in a store to learn every aspect of store management before an outlet is allocated to them.

For more information about becoming a franchisee call Andy Cooke on 01908 580 656 or e-mail franchise.sales@dominos.co.uk. Further information is also available at www.dominos.uk.com.

Kall Kwik

Founded in 1978 and a nationwide business, Kall Kwik is a leading force in the business-to-business print, digital and design sector.

To be successful in Kall Kwik you need selling skills and the ability to establish and develop relationships with key clients. It is those fundamental abilities that allow franchisees to offer bespoke business solutions and achieve the high-margin sales that allow investment back into the business as it develops and grows.

A prime example is Kall Kwik Edinburgh and Paisley. It is an award-winning centre run by Mark and Jemima McCluskey, a husband-and-wife business partnership. They bought the existing Kall Kwik centre in Edinburgh in March 1995 and focused their energies on fostering strong links with the local business community. They added to their thriving business by investing in the latest production techniques and expanding the size of their premises. In their first two years of business their sales grew from £350,000 to £630,000, and in eight years they added £1 million to their turnover, and moved up Kall Kwik's national performance table from 120th to seventh place. In 2003, they won first prize in the BFA Franchisee of the Year awards.

Today, the couple own two Kall Kwik centres, in Edinburgh and Paisley, and two years ago they invested in a 3,500 square foot central production unit. Their business expansion has also greatly improved the working environment for their staff, who are one of their greatest assets and have helped them experience significant sales growth.

Another example of a sales-focused success story is Kall Kwik in Bishop's Stortford in Hertfordshire, which has been revolutionised by its owner Fred Lane since he bought it in 2001. His strong sales ethos secured lucrative contracts with blue chip companies and turned the centre into one of the fastest growing in the network.

Award winners Mark and Jemima McCluskey

His team of six professionals, ranging from designers to customer service personnel, work on a variety of accounts including Peak Fitness, Pearson Education, GlaxoSmithKline, FedEx, easyJet and Air Harrods.

The centre is currently working with Business Link towards the prestigious Investors in People accreditation. Fred has invested in new technology, and with a strong team behind him, is passionate about growing the business through sales, marketing development and attention to customer services. With an MBA and a background in multinational companies, he embodies the ambition, sales focus and hard-working nature needed to make a success of a franchised business.

Kall Kwik has been around long enough to be a family tradition. The Kall Kwik Digital Business Centre in the City of London was set-up by cousins Richard Adler and David Marks, who are the sons of the two Kall Kwik franchise families who have served the City for 20 years from their centres in High Holborn and Southampton Row. The Digital

The Kall Kwik Digital Business Centre in London

Centre was opened in August 2002 and over the following year sales grew 260 per cent thanks to a high profile client portfolio including Nasdaq, Aquascutum, Pret a Manger, the London Stock Exchange and Lloyd's of London. The centre has invested more than £300,000 in cutting-edge digital technology such as Xerox Docucolor 2060, a high volume digital press, and a Canon BJW9000 large format colour ink jet printer.

In Bristol, Kall Kwik owners Chris and Linda Mills achieved a record year with a turnover of £1 million. Their centre in Gloucester Road is one of the most successful in the network. No stranger to overseeing successful business operations, Chris Mills was divisional sales manager for Yellow Pages and Thomson Directories before taking up the Kall Kwik centre some 12 years ago. Since then, he and Linda have significantly grown their enterprise by adding a second centre in Fairfax Street, Bristol, and a third in Bath. They hope to maximise profits by sharing their production resources between the three centres. Over the last couple of years, they have invested £250,000 in a full-colour printing press to meet the increasingly complex creative needs of their customers.

Chris and Linda credit their success to a clear consistent strategy that focuses on business-to-business sales, a dedicated sales team and strong support received from Kall Kwik UK.

The couple follow a targeted marketing strategy through the use of direct mail and regularly promoting their business communication services to local companies and organisations. But the real secret of their success is that clients are so loyal, coming back time and again because they are offered unique business solutions and consistently excellent service – prime example of the key attributes of success within Kall Kwik.

If you come from a sales background or have good client relationship skills, you may wish to consider Kall Kwik as a franchising opportunity. New locations are being established throughout the country and there are also opportunities to acquire existing businesses as current franchisees seek retirement. Contact Kall Kwik UK: 0500 872 060 or log onto: www.kallkwik.co.uk.

The Kall Kwik branding

Rainbow International

Towards the end of 1999, Jim Kerr decided to start his own company. He began looking around for a suitable project and his search led him to the British Franchise Association. They supplied him with a wealth of information on franchising in general and a list of approved organisations that were seeking new franchisees.

His search began in earnest as he investigated around 20 companies before deciding in the early part of 2000 on restoration and cleaning company Rainbow International. His induction training began in April 2000. So what drew him to Rainbow International? This is his story in his own words:

> I had absolutely no experience in carpet and upholstery cleaning or fire and flood restoration before joining Rainbow International. My background was mainly in the police, the military, diplomatic protection, and for a while I even owned a pub.
>
> The reason I chose Rainbow International over all the other franchises I looked at was because I could see that I could build a real business with their help instead of just creating a job for myself.
>
> At Rainbow International's head office I spent a whole day with the managing director, Melvin Lusty and franchise recruitment manager, Ron Hutton, and found them to be marketing driven and focused. They had a real vision of what they wanted Rainbow International to become and how they could get it to that point. They were also able to show me exactly how I fitted into their plans and what I could expect from a Rainbow International franchise.
>
> I started with one technician and we went through induction training together. The training was thorough and professional and

by the end we were confident that we could provide a top-level service to our customers.

Ongoing training and support is a big part of the Rainbow International system, and whenever we are unsure of how to proceed with a technical matter or a business related matter, help is literally a phone call away.

Jim Kerr (left) with Melvin Lusty, Managing Director, Rainbow International

Four years later, I have a team of people, a fleet of vehicles, a 4,000 square foot industrial unit and enough equipment to take on the biggest jobs with no difficulty.

In the early days I was very hands-on. I was literally involved in every job we did, which was vital to gain the knowledge and experience that only comes through seeing and doing the job yourself. Now, I only get personally involved in technically challenging jobs and spend the vast majority of my time working 'on' the business rather than 'in' it. This is crucial if you want to build a successful business for yourself.

Success has come about quite simply by following the Rainbow International system, which focuses on customer satisfaction, investment in staff training and wellbeing, and reinvestment of profits into better equipment and premises. There are no easy rides; you must be committed to the growth and development of both your business and, in particular, your people, who are your greatest business asset.

By following the Rainbow International system I have built a solid and enduring business, which continues to function and earn money whether I am there or not. I have not yet finished growing my business and fine-tuning our operational procedures, and I look forward with confidence to the years ahead, secure in the knowledge that I am part of an organisation that is committed to my success.

I put plenty of time and effort into researching a number of franchise opportunities before choosing Rainbow International. I chose well.

Rainbow International was established in the UK in 1987 and provides a wide range of restoration, repair and cleaning services for homes and commercial premises through a network of over 120 multi-personnel, multi-vehicle branches.

Under the stewardship of Melvin Lusty, Rainbow International has developed into a much sought-after franchise opportunity in the UK and a market leader in claims management and restoration services to the insurance industry. The company delivers a comprehensive portfolio of

Case study: Rainbow International

Rainbow International to the rescue

fire, flood and accidental damage restoration services on behalf of the UK's top insurance companies and all major loss adjusters nationwide. Its head office is in Mansfield, Nottinghamshire.

Rainbow International has reached the finals of the British Franchise Association Franchisor of the Year Awards four times, finally taking the top prize in 2001. Nor have its franchisees gone unnoticed, with first place in the Franchisee of the Year Award in 1999 and third in 2001. The company is a full BFA member and holds the Investor in People standard.

Rainbow International is part of the Dwyer Group, a Texas-based, worldwide franchise organisation supporting over 1,200 franchisees in 24 countries. In the UK, Rainbow International is owned and operated under licence to the Dwyer Group by ISS Damage Control, part of the ISS (Integrated Service Solutions) Group.

ISS offers business customers worldwide a range of services including damage control, cleaning, security, maintenance and electrics, reception, landscaping, pest control and catering. With its backing, Rainbow International has made its services extremely attractive to loss adjusting firms and insurance companies.

Rainbow International continues to seek ambitious franchisees who are motivated business managers and have the desire, commitment and commercial acumen to grow and develop million-pound businesses in an ever-changing, demanding, yet rewarding industry.

Prospective franchisees require an investment of approximately £30,000, and approximately £20,000 working capital, which covers the exclusive area license, training, machinery, tools, IT hardware and software and a full marketing pack. For more information about the Rainbow International franchise, log on to www.rainbow-int.co.uk, contact Ron Hutton on 01623 675100 or e-mail ron@rainbow-int.co.uk.

Appendices

Appendix I
Understanding company accounts

If knowledge is power, then it pays prospective franchisees to find out as much as possible about companies that interest them. All limited liability companies are required by law to produce a set of accounts, and much can be gleaned by going through them carefully. They are not, however, guaranteed to be crystal clear. Just as there are many ways of skinning a cat, should you wish to do such a thing, there are a variety of ways of presenting a company's picture through its figures. So an ability to read between the lines comes in handy. Also, a figure in isolation, like a cat without its skin, means little. To get at the meaning of accounts, you need to look at **trends**, by comparing figures over a period of time, and at **ratios**, by comparing one figure with another in the same period.

Although different companies present their accounts in different ways, three basic features are common to them all. Each must have a **balance sheet**, a **profit and loss account**, and a **cash flow statement**. And each of these tells you something about the health of the business.

The balance sheet

The balance sheet is a snapshot of a company's worth on one particular day, the last day of its financial year. In most cases it gives the best opportunity to make an assessment of the shape the company is in. However, just as an enthusiastic drinker may be adept at hiding the truth from his doctor, it is not unknown for a company to bring forward some items or delay others to give a rosy glow to the balance sheet, a technique known as window dressing.

The balance sheet tells you what the company owns, its **asset**s, and what it owes, its **liabilities**. There are two kinds of assets – fixed and current. Fixed assets are long-term items such as land, buildings and machinery, and intangibles such as brand names and goodwill. Current assets are shorter term and include cash, stocks, debtors (money owed to the company): all the things, in short, that a business needs for its day-to-day running.

Liabilities, too, are divided into the short and long term. Current, or short-term, liabilities are usually debts that must be paid within a year; most of these are owed to suppliers, the company's creditors. Longer-term liabilities include items such as bank loans and corporate bonds where payment is due after a year.

Subtract the current liabilities from the current assets and you get a good idea of how solvent the company is in the short term. A large positive figure is a healthy sign, a much smaller one, or worse a negative figure, and the patient is giving cause for concern. Current assets divided by current liabilities gives you the **liquidity ratio**, a good way of spotting whether the patient has been at the bottle. A ratio of one means current assets equal current liabilities, a sign that a company may not have enough cash to meet its debts in the coming year. Anything less than one is bad news. Better still is the acid test, which strips stocks out of current assets side of the equation (because they may be difficult to sell, or even give away), and therefore gives a brutally frank indication of the company's ability to settle its short-term debts if they were all called in today. A ratio of less than one is an alarm bell bordering on the deafening. Subtract current liabilities from total assets and you get capital employed. If you now take operating profit (found on the profit and loss statement) and divide it by capital employed you get **return on capital employed**, a favourite device for measuring company profitability.

The profit and loss statement

Unlike the snapshot picture given by the balance sheet, the profit and loss statement shows the results of a company's trading over a defined period, usually a year.

The first figure is **turnover**, or the total value of all sales of goods and services made by the company. Turnover minus cost of sales (the cost incurred by the company throughout the year on everything that forms part of the finished goods) gives **gross profit**. Next, after overheads such as marketing and distribution are deducted, you have **operating profit**. The notes to the accounts, which are well worth a close look, give a greater insight into costs such as directors' remuneration, expenditure on research and development, and depreciation. The next deduction is the interest the company pays on its borrowings. (A big payment could be a sign of trouble. If so, look again at the liquidity ratio and acid test outlined in the section under balance sheet.) When the interest is deducted you are left with **pre-tax profit**, the most commonly quoted measure of a company's profit. After the taxman has had his cut (corporation tax is charged at 30 per cent on profits of more than £1.5 million), you are left with **net profit**, which, generally speaking, belongs to the shareholders. The company decides how much of this should be distributed as dividends and how much should be held as retained earnings to help fund future growth.

The cashflow statement

Taken together, retained earnings and depreciation (money put back into the business for the specific purpose of allowing for wear and tear on plant and equipment) are called **cashflow**. Both are money retained out of profits for the future needs of a company. Cash is now seen as such a vital item in a company's accounts (firms can go bust, not because they are failing to produce goods and services that people want, but because they run out of money) that it is a legal requirement to include a cashflow statement in the report and accounts as well as a profit and loss statement.

The first line on the cashflow statement is net cash inflow from operating activities. This is the ready cash that a company generates from its trading through the year. The next section, returns on investments and servicing of finance, mainly covers interest paid and received. Then comes a taxation section, which covers corporation tax paid. After that, the statement moves from revenue to capital items under a section headed capital expenditure and financial investment, which shows the sum spent on acquiring fixed assets or received from selling such assets.

Now all the cash inflows and outflows are added up and weighed against each other to give either **net cash inflow** or **net cash outflow**. The final line shows the increase or decrease in the cash held by the company over the year. The cashflow statement tells you how well a company is financing its investment and shows if its cash resources are under pressure. If you take the cash from operating activities, interest received and so on, and deduct the cash paid out in interest charges, tax, and dividends, you can see whether the company is generating sufficient cash to cover its running costs.

Appendix II
Selling

Effective sales techniques

There is something about the very thought of selling that strikes fear into the hearts of many British people. As with most phobias, the causes are largely non-specific, but an aversion to selling probably has a lot to do with (a) a fear of rejection and (b) a dislike of the bullying, foot-in-the-door persistence that caricatures the salesman at his worst.

For franchisees there is bad news and good. The bad is that some form of selling is vital to the success of any business, for the simple and obvious reason that an enterprise without sales is like a balloon without air. The good news is that hard selling is seldom required. (However, if you happen to be blessed with the kind of bold nature that allows you to 'cold call' strangers and walk away from a rebuff unfazed and with enthusiasm undiminished, good luck to you. You should go far.) Even better news: the sense of offended propriety that makes you recoil from the foot-in-the-door salesman is, in a sense, the key to making a success of your business. For it implies that you value the opposite characteristics of courtesy, politeness, consideration and an appreciation of the other person's point of view – all great attributes when it comes to promoting your business, winning new customers and keeping existing ones.

An open, honest, and friendly attitude is a natural form of salesmanship possessed by fortunate people who would shrink from the idea of themselves as sellers. So the first rule of selling is to remember that it is part of everything you do in your business. To be prompt, to be polite, to smile, to answer the phone in a friendly welcoming way, to deal quickly with inquiries and efficiently with complaints – these are all effective sales techniques. You must adopt them and, if you employ staff, you should ensure that they, too, know the meaning of service and customer satisfaction.

Know your product or service

The second rule of selling is to know your product or service and, if necessary, be able to demonstrate it. The more knowledgeable and enthusiastic you are about what it is you are selling and the benefits it confers, the more you will discover the natural salesperson that slept unsuspected within you.

Know your customer

There are other rules about selling that are organisational and mainly a matter of common sense. For example, you should keep a record of your customers, stay in touch with them, and listen to what they have to say. The closer you can get to them without being pushy the better chance you stand of winning repeat orders and getting word-of-mouth recommendation – there is no better form of advertising.

Marketing

Selling is a part of marketing, which is the process of finding customers and meeting their needs. When Ralph Waldo Emerson said, 'if a man make a better mousetrap than his neighbour, though he build his house in the woods, the world will make a beaten path to his door' he was not entirely right. For the world to sit up and take notice in the manner prescribed, it must first know the better mousetrap has been invented and secondly where in the woods the inventor is to be found. In the absence of an informed market, the shed will remain full of unsold rodent snares. So the inventor must don the cap of marketer and find out who in the neighbourhood has mice and how best to bring his invention to their notice. Basic stuff, but essential all the same. The franchisee must, therefore, constantly bear in mind what it is that his or her business has to offer; who are the likely customers; who is the competition; and what is the best way of getting the product or service known.

A good and experienced franchisor will be able to offer a lot of help with marketing and include it as a subject in the initial training course. After all, he or she has already established that a market exists and has tried and tested the best means of reaching it.

Advertising

As we have seen, advertising, a powerful tool in the right hands, will probably be carried out by the franchisor on behalf, and at the expense of, all the franchisees – the aim, primarily, being to promote the brand nationally. That does not rule out local advertising and promotion by the franchisees in their own areas and at their own expense. In fact, such activity is usually essential. Advertising in the local press, the *Yellow Pages*, and leafleting are well-used and successful means of getting a local business known.

Cold calling

As for the more direct approach of knocking on potential customers' doors or contacting them by phone (the activities dreaded by people for whom selling holds the appeal of bathing in a pool full of pirhanas), again the franchisor should be able to help, often by example. It is not unusual for new franchisees to be accompanied by experienced sales people 'in the field' (a term borrowed from the military which carries the right connotations of an organised campaign to achieve victory but the wrong ones of blood and bullets, items seldom encountered by even the most obnoxious double glazing salesman). Just as apprentices learnt most by observing the craftsmen at work, the inexperienced franchisee can learn more about selling by being with a professional for a week than reading about it for a month.

That said, there are a few ground rules for cold calling by telephone that are worth bearing in mind:

- **Find a quiet place** where you can talk without interruption. If possible use a hands-free phone to allow you to make notes.
- **Compile a list** of prospects, their names and job titles.
- **Rehearse** your opening line. Say who you are and why you are calling. Establish quickly if there is an interest in your product or service.
- **Have all the facts** at your fingertips – how much your goods or services cost; how many have already been sold; why they are better than your competitors'; their specifications and availability; delivery times; and so on. Have your fax and mobile phone numbers, email addresses and postcodes to hand and your diary at your elbow.
- Be sure to **get something out of the call**, even if it's only striking that particular prospect from your list. Things to aim for are a face-to-face meeting, a request for a brochure, or an agreement to call again at a future date.
- **Follow through**. Make a note of the conversation and be sure to deliver what you promised, and quickly. Get the brochure in the post. Send any information requested.

Practice makes perfect

The above is only a sketchy guide to the business of selling. The best way to learn is through practice. You'll be surprised how your confidence grows each time you meet a prospect and enthuse about your product or service. You may find, to your amazement, that you actually enjoy it. Of all the many rewards of running and building a business, few compare with the sheer exhilaration of clinching a sale and knowing you did it through your own efforts. The watchwords are to **know your products** and **respect your customers**.

Appendix III
The British Franchise Association members

The following information has been kindly supplied by the British Franchise Association. The publishers cannot be held responsible for any errors or omissions.

Full members

The following are established franchisors with a proven trading and franchising record. To qualify as a full member, franchisors are required to submit a completed application form, including disclosure document, franchise agreement, prospectus and accounts, and proof of a correctly constituted pilot scheme successfully operated for at least one year, financed and managed by the applicant company. In addition, evidence of successful franchising over a subsequent two-year period with at least four franchisees is required.

Abacus Care
Care service provider
Ormskirk Business Park
71/73 New Court Way
Ormskirk L39 2YT
Contact: Ian McDougall
Tel: 01695 585 400
Fax: 01695 585 401
headoffice@abacuscare.com

Alldays Stores
Convenience stores
Alldays House, 1 Chestnut Avenue
Chandlers Ford, Eastleigh SO53 3HJ
Contact: Paul Criddle
Tel: 023 8064 5315
pcriddle@alldays.co.uk

Alphagraphics
Rapid response print, copy and publishing stores
Thornburgh Road
Eastfield, Scarborough YO11 3UY
www.alphagraphics.co.uk
Contact: Beverley Bolton
Tel: 01723 502222
s.campbell@alphagraphics.co.uk

Amtrak Express Parcels
Overnight parcels collection and delivery
Northgate Way
Northgate, Aldridge
Walsall, W Mids WS9 8ST
Contact: David Scott
Tel: 01922 744474
Fax: 01922 743140
franchise.dept@amtrak.co.uk

ANC
Express parcel delivery
Parkhouse East Industrial Estate
Chesterton, Newcastle-under-Lyme
Staffs ST5 7RB
Contact: John Hamill
Tel: 01782 563322
Fax: 01782 563633
franchise@anc.co.uk

Apetito Ltd (Wiltshire Farm Foods)
Home meals for the elderly and infirm
Canal Road
Trowbridge, Wilts BA14 8RJ
Contact: Gary Rigby
Tel: 01225 756074
Fax: 01225 756069
gary.rigby@apetito.co.uk

Apollo Window Blinds
Manufacturers and retailers of window blinds
Unit 10b, Park View Industrial Estate
Hartlepool, Teesside TS25 1PE
www.apollo-blinds.co.uk
Contact: Graham Mylchreest
Tel: 01429 851500
Fax: 01429 851529
franchising@apollo-blinds.co.uk

Auditel
Cost management consultants
St Paul, Cross Street
Winchester, Hants SO23 8SZ
www.era-auditel.net
Contact: Robert Allison
Tel: 01962 863915
kate@era-auditel.net

Bang & Olufsen
Retail television & hi-fi
630 Wharfedale Road
Winnersh Triangle
Wokingham, Berks RG41 5TP
Contact: Mr D Mottershead
Tel: 0118 969 2288
cev@bang-olufsen.dk

BB's Coffee & Muffins Limited
Fast food
Charter House, Brent Way
Brentford, Mddx TW8 8ES
Tel: 020 8758 1234
Fax: 020 8568 6868
Contact: Mr N Sidhu
Tel: 020 8758 1234
Fax: 020 8568 6868
franchise@bbscoffeeandmuffins.com

Belvoir Lettings
Property management and residential letting
Belvoir House
Grantham, Lincs NG31 6HR
www.belvoirfranchise.com
Contact: Mr M Goddard
Tel: 01476 570000
Fax: 01476 584902
franchising@belvoirlettings.com

BIGFISH
Office printer supplies and printer repairs
Caslon Court, Pitronnerie Road
St Peter Port, Guernsey GY1 2RW
www.bigfishfranchise.com
Contact: Mark Holland
Tel: 0771 532 6717
Fax: 01604 677502
mark.holland@bigfishfranchise.com

Blazes Fireplace Centres
Fireplace and fire retailers
Signature House, 21 Parker Street
Burnley, Lancs BB11 1AP
www.blazes.co.uk
Contact: Mr M Eyre
Tel: 01282 831176
info@blazes.co.uk

Card Connection
Greeting card publisher and distributor
Park House, South Street
Farnham, Surrey GU9 7QQ
www.card-connection.co.uk
Contact: Robina Every
Tel: 01252 892200
ho@card-connection.co.uk

Card Line Greetings
Distribution of greetings cards
Units 4–5 Hale Trading Estate
Lower Church Lane
Tipton, W Mids DY4 7PQ
www.cardline.co.uk
Contact: Mr M Crapper
Tel: 0121 522 4407
info@cardline.co.uk

Carewatch Care Services
Domiciliary care services
54–56 West Street
Brighton, E Sussex BN1 2SE
Contact: Patrick Thompson
Tel: 01273 208111
Fax: 01273 204111
recruitment@carewatch.co.uk

Cash Converters
Buying and selling second-hand goods
Cash Converters House,
Westmill Road
Ware, Herts SG12 0EF
Contact: Julian Urry
Tel: 01920 485696
Fax: 01920 485695
caroline.barber@cashconverters.net

Cash Generator
Second-hand goods, instant cash provider, cheque changer
63/64 Oakhill Trading Estate,
Worsley Road North
Walkden M28 3PT
www.cashgenerator.net
Contact: Mr B C Lewis
Tel: 01204 574444
Fax: 01204 577711
info@cashgenerator.co.uk

Castle Estates
Residential property management
10 Merrick Way
Chandlers, Eastleigh SO53 4QT
www.franchise.castle-estates.co.uk
Contact: Mike Edwards
Tel: 02380 270025
Fax: 0870 839 2728
franchise@castle-estates.co.uk

Certax Accounting
Accountancy and taxation services
47 Clarence Road
Chesterfield, Derbys S40 1LQ
www.certax.co.uk
Contact: Keith Bradshaw
Tel: 01246 200255
Fax: 01246 279403
CA@certax.co.uk

Chem Dry Midlands & London
Carpet, upholstery and curtain cleaning
Unit 3, Kettlebrook Road
Tamworth, Staffs B77 1AG
www.chem-dry.co.uk
Contact: Sally Jaggs
Tel: 01827 723988
Fax: 01827 723989
info@chemdry.org.uk

Chem Dry Northern & Southern
Belprin Road
Beverley, E Yorks HU17 0LP
Tel: 01482 888195
Fax: 01482 888193
www.chem-dry.co.uk
Contact: Claire Hostick
Tel: 01482 888195
Fax: 01482 888193
info@cdns.co.uk

Chemex International
Hygiene, cleaning and maintenance chemicals
Spring Road
Smethwick, W Mids B66 1PT
www.chemexinter.com
Contact: Mr L J Gray
Tel: 0121 525 4040
Fax: 0121 525 4919
chemex@chemicalexpress.co.uk

Choice Hotels
Hotelier
Premier House
112/114 Station Road
Edgeware, Mddx HA8 7BJ
Contact: Richard Arman
Tel: 0208 233 2001
Fax: 0208 233 2000
richardarman@choicehotelseurope.com

Clarks Shoes
Retail shoe shops
40 High Street
Street, Somerset BA16 OYA
Contact: Mr R Marsden
Tel: 01458 443131
roger.marsden@clarks.com

Colorworks Auto Services
Automotive paint repairs
8 Regent Place
Rugby, Warks CV21 2YU
Tel: 01788 569999
Fax: 01788 570080
www.colorworksonline.co.uk
Contact: Mrs Terry Nicholson
Tel: 0800 917 4379
color-works@btconnect.com

Colour Counsellors
Interior decorating
3 Dovedale Studios,
465 Battersea Park Road
London SW11 4LR
www.colourcounsellors.co.uk
Contact: Mrs V Stourton
Tel: 0207 978 5023
info@colourcounsellors.co.uk

Complete Weed Control
Weed control services
Hackling House,
Bourton Industrial Park
Bourton-on-the-Water,
Glos GL54 2EN
Tel: 01451 822897
Fax: 01451 822587
Contact: Roger Turner
Tel: 01451 822897
Fax: 01451 822587
roger.turner@completeweedcontrol.co.uk

Cottage Industries
Distribution of greeting cards and confectionery
399A Harrogate Road
Bradford, Yorks BD2 3TF
Contact: Mr A Cheetham
Tel: 01274 626556
info@cottageindustries.co.uk

Countrywide Grounds Maintenance
Grounds maintenance contractors
Teejay Court, Alderley Road
Wilmslow, Cheshire SK9 1NT
Tel: 01625 529000
Fax: 01625 527000
www.countrywidegrounds.co.uk/franchise
Contact: Simon Stott
Tel: 01625 529000
Fax: 01625 527000
franchise@countrywidegrounds.co.uk

Domino's Pizza
Home delivery and takeaway pizza
Lasborough Road
Kingston, Milton Keynes
MK10 0AB
Contact: Beth Stedman
Tel: 01908 580617
BethS@dominos.co.uk

DP Furniture Express
Pine furniture retailer
Colima Avenue, Sunderland
Enterprise Park
Sunderland, Tyne & Wear
SR5 3XF
Tel: 0191 516 2600
Fax: 0191 549 6304
www.durhampine.com
Contact: Lex Spence
Tel: 0191 516 2600
Fax: 0191 549 6304
lex.spence@dp-fx.com

Drain Doctor
Plumbing
Franchise House, Adam Court
Newark Road, Peterborough
Cambs PE1 5PP
www.draindoctor.co.uk
Contact: Mr F S Mitman
Tel: 01733 753939
jan.mitman@virgin.net

Driver Hire
Employment agency
Progress House, Castlefields Lane
Bingley, W Yorks BD16 2AB
www.driver-hire.co.uk
Contact: Nichola Watson
Tel: 01274 551166
info@driver-hire.co.uk

Dyno-Locks
Lock fitting and security
Zockoll House, 143 Maple Road
Surbiton, Surrey KT6 4BJ
www.dyno.com
Contact: Franchise recruitment department
Tel: 0500 456267
franchiserecruitment@dyno.com

Dyno-Rod
Drain cleaning
Zockoll House, 143 Maple Road
Surbiton, Surrey KT6 4BJ
www.dyno.com
Contact: Franchise recruitment department
Tel: 0500 456267
franchiserecruitment@dyno.com

Ecocleen Limited
Commercial cleaning
3 Northgate Street
Bury St Edmunds, Suffolk IP33 1HQ
Contact: Peter Legge
Tel: 01284 703535
Fax: 01284 700180
atraher@ecocleen.co.uk

Express Dairies
Dairy products
Fosse House, 6 Smith Way
Grove Park, Leicester LE9 5SX
Contact: Mike Grey
Tel: 0116 281 6281
Fax: 0116 282 1202
mike-grey@express-dairies.co.uk

Favorite Chicken & Ribs
Fast food
7 Davy Road, Gorse Lane
Clacton-on-Sea, Essex CO15 4XD
Contact: Adrian Goody
Tel: 01255 222568
Fax: 01255 430423
mailroom@favorite.co.uk

The Flat Roof Company
Refurbishment of flat roofs
Unit 7, Guardian Park
Station Industrial Estate
Tadcaster, N Yorks LS24 9SG
www.flatroof.co.uk
Contact: Kevin Moody
Tel: 01937 530788
franchise@flatroof.co.uk

Francesco Group
Hairdressing
1 The Green
Stafford ST17 4BH
Contact: Mr F Dellicompagni
Tel: 01785 247175
Fax: 01785 216185
headoffice@francescogroup.co.uk

Freedom Group of Companies
Facilities management
Freedom House, Bradford Road
Tingley, Wakefield WF3 1SD
www.freedom-group.co.uk
Contact: Michele Glover
Tel: 01924 887785
michele.glover@freedom-group.co.uk

Guardian Homecare
Domiciliary care services
Hamilton House, 2 Station Road
Epping, Essex CM16 4HA
Contact: Anne Keene
Tel: 01992 575666
Fax: 01992 575152
jan.guardian@rya-online.net

Hire Intelligence
Computer rental
Unit 2, Goldhawk Estate
2A Brackenbury Road
Hammersmith, London W6 0BA
Contact: Mr Ruediger Feiler
Tel: 020 8544 9840
Fax: 0208 740 4004
wrfeiler@hire-intelligence.co.uk

Initial City Link
Parcel collection & delivery
Wellington House, 61/73 Staines Road West
Sudbury on Thames, Mddx
TW16 7AH
www.city-link.co.uk
Contact: Mr Chris Johnson
Tel: 01932 822622
Fax: 01932 785560
linda.brown@city-link.co.uk

Interlink Express Parcels
Parcel collection & delivery
PO Box 6979, Roebuck Lane
Smethwick, Warley, W Mids
B66 1BY
Contact: Mike Noad
Tel: 01562 881002
Fax: 01562 881001
jane.hodgkinson@geopostuk.com

In-Toto
Kitchen and bathroom furniture and appliances
Shaw Cross Court,
Shaw Cross Business Park
Dewsbury, W Yorks WF12 7RF
www.intotofranchise.co.uk
Contact: Mr D Watts
Tel: 01937 841483 mob 07785 552541
david.watts@intoto.co.uk

Jo Jingles
Music and singing club for pre-school children
Myrtle House
Nr Amersham, Bucks HP7 0PX
Contact: Mrs Gill Thomas
Tel: 01494 719360
Fax: 01494 719361
headoffice@jojingles.co.uk

Kall-Kwik Printing
Quick printing
ODC, 106 Pembroke Road
Ruislip, Mddx HA4 8NW
www.kallkwik.co.uk
Contact: Louise Robertson
Tel: 01895 872000
Fax: 01895 872110
louise.robertson@odclimited.com

Kumon Educational
After-school tuition
Fifth Floor, The Grange
100 High Street
London N14 6BN
Tel: 020 8447 9010
Fax: 020 8447 9030
Contact: Carl Davies
Tel: 020 8447 9010
Fax: 020 8447 9030
info@kumon.co.uk

Legal & General Franchising
Estate agency, lettings, sales & management
68 School Road
Tilehurst, Reading
Berks RG31 5AW
Contact: Michael Stoop
Tel: 0118 945 9900
Fax: 0118 945 9901
admin@lgfl.co.uk

Martin & Co
Property management & lettings
182 Old Christchurch Road
Bournemouth BH1 1NU
www.propertyfranchise.co.uk
Contact: Christine Hanson
Tel: 01202 292829
chris.hanson@martinco.com

McDonald's
Fast food
11–59 High Road
East Finchley, London N2 8AW
Contact: Franchising team
Tel: 020 8700 7153
Fax: 0181 700 7469
franchise@uk.mcd.com

Metro Rod
Drain care and repair
Metro House, Churchill Way
Macclesfield, Cheshire SK11 6AY
Tel: 01625 888131
Fax: 01625 616687
www.metrorod.co.uk
Contact: Wendy Drennan
Tel: 01625 888131
Fax: 01625 616687
wendy.drennan@metrorod.co.uk

Minster Services Group
Contract cleaning
Minster House,
948–952 Kingsbury Road
Erdington, Birmingham B24 9PZ
www.minstergroup.co.uk
Contact: Alan Haigh
Tel: 0121 386 1722
minster@minstergroup.co.uk

Molly Maid
Domestic cleaning
Bishop House South,
The Bishop Centre
Bath Road
Taplow, Maidenhead SL6 ONY
www.mollymaid.co.uk/franchise
Contact: Pam Bader
Tel: 01628 663500
Fax: 01628 663700
rmaidment@mollymaid.co.uk

Mr Clutch
Fast fit of clutches, gearboxes and brakes
2 Priory Road
Stroud, Rochester, Kent ME2 2EG
Contact: Joe Yussuf
Tel: 01634 717747
Fax: 01634 731115

Mr Electric
Electrical installation and repair
Five Mile House, 128 Hanbury Road
Bromsgrove, Worcs B60 4JZ
Contact: Clive Houlston
Tel: 01527 574343
Fax: 01527 874301
enquiries@mr-electric.co.uk

MRI Worldwide
Executive recruitment
MRI House, 5 Victoria Street
Windsor, Berks SL4 1HB
www.mriww.com
Contact: Brett Cooper
Tel: 0870 777 3900
Fax: 0870 777 3910
bcooper@mriww.com

National Schoolwear Centres
Schoolwear retail
Ketteringham Hall, Church Road
Wymondham, Norfolk NR18 9RS
Tel: 01603 819966
Fax: 01603 819977
Contact: Ian Masson
Tel: 01603 819966
Fax: 01603 819977
ianm@n-sc.co.uk

Nationwide Investigations Group
Private investigations bureau
141 Western Road
Haywards Heath, W Sussex
RH16 3LH
Tel: 01444 416004
Fax: 01444 441663
www.nig.co.uk
Contact: Mr S Withers
Tel: 01444 416004
Fax: 01444 441663
franchise@nig.co.uk

O'Briens Irish Sandwich Bars
Sandwich cafes
2 Elsinore House,
77 Fulham Palace Road
London W6 8JA
www.obriens.ie
Contact: Paul Stanton
Tel: 0113 2470444
Fax: 0113 2470555
info@obriens.ie

The Original Poster Company
Distribution of greeting cards
Elephant House, 28 Lyon Road
Walton on Thames, Surrey KT12 3PU
www.originalposter.com
Contact: Jeremy Webster
Tel: 01932 267300
Fax: 01932 267333
fionar@originalposter.com

Ovenu
Oven cleaning
67 Barkham Ride
Wokingham, Berks RG40 4HA
Contact: Rik Hallewell
Tel: 01189 736 739
Fax: 01189 731 876
rik.ovenu@ukonline.co.uk

PDC International
Quick printing
1 Church Lane
East Grinstead, W Sussex RH19 3AZ
www.pdccopyprint.co.uk
Contact: Stephen Ricketts
Tel: 01342 315321
pdc@pdc-intl.demon.co.uk

Perfect Pizza
Fast food
Units 5 & 6 The Forum
Hanworth Lane
Chertsey, Surrey KT16 9JX
www.perfectpizza.co.uk
Contact: Louise Benjamin
Tel: 01932 568000
louise_benjamin@perfectpizza.co.uk

Pirtek Europe
Hydraulic and industrial hoses
35 Acton Park Estate, The Vale
Acton, London W3 7QE
Contact: John Chaplin
Tel: 020 8 749 8444
info@pirtekuk.com

Pitman Training Group
Office skills training
Pitman House, Audby Lane
Wetherby, W Yorks LS22 7FD
www.pitman-training.co.uk
Contact: Mr M Graham
Tel: 01937 548500
franchising-opportunities@
pitman-training.com

Post Office Ltd
Retail and Post Office products
Franchise Opportunities
Prospero House,
241 Borough High Street
London SE1 1GG
Contact: Stephanie Lawrie
Tel: 0207 9407627
Fax: 0207 9407637
POL_Franchise_Opportunities@
postoffice.co.uk

Primary Books
Children's books
The Old Diary, High Street, Grateley
Andover, Hants SP11 8JS
Contact: Anne Phillips
Tel: 01264 889000
Fax: 01624 889900
annephillips@primarybooks.co.uk

Prontaprint
Quick print
106 Pembroke Road
Ruislip, Mddx HA4 8NW
www.prontaprint.com
Contact: Louise Robertson
Tel: 01895 872064
Fax: 01895 872110
louise.robertson@odclimited.com

Pronuptia Bridal & Mens Formal Wear
Dress hire
PO Box 2478
Hove BN3 6AG
Tel: 01273 563006
Fax: 01273 563006
Contact: Robert Devlin
Tel: 01273 563006
Fax: 01273 563006
pronuptia@btopenworld.com

The Property Search Group
Property services for the legal sector
Stonecrest, 9 Sandbeds
Huddersfield, W Yorks HD7 2RD
Contact: Mr Gary Hester
Tel: 01484 311649
Fax: 01484 311539
info@propertysearchgroup.co.uk

Rainbow International
Carpet care and restoration
Spectrum House, Lower Oakham Way
Oakham Business Park, Mansfield
NG18 5BY
www.rainbow-int.co.uk
Contact: Ron Hutton
Tel: 01623 675100
ron@rainbow-int.co.uk

Recognition Express
Name badges and signage
Wheatfield Way, Hinckley Fields
Hinckley, Leics LE10 1YG
www.recognition-express.com/franchise/
Contact: Mr N Toplis
Tel: 01455 445555
Fax: 01455 445566
franchise@recognition-express.com

Rosemary Conley Diet and Fitness Clubs
Quorn House, Meeting Street
Quorn, Loughborough, Leics
LE12 8EX
www.rosemary-conley.co.uk
Contact: Heather Shaw
Tel: 01509 620222
Heather.Shaw@rosemary-conley.co.uk

Safeclean
Furniture care and stain removal
152 Milton Park
Abingdon, Oxon OX14 4SD
Contact: Paul Roberts
Tel: 01235 444757
safeclean@valspar.com

Saks Hair & Beauty
Hairdressing
Saks Franchise Services
Saks HQ, 55–59 Duke Street
Darlington DL3 7SD
www.sakshairandbeauty.com
Contact: Jennifer Evans
Tel: 01325 380333
Fax: 01325 360228
franchise@sakshairandbeauty.com

Scottish & Newcastle Pub Enterprises
Public houses
2–4 Broadway Place, South Gyle
Broadway
Edinburgh EH12 9JZ
www.pub-enterprises.co.uk
Contact: Kay Sibbald
Tel: Freephone 0500 94 95 96 or
0131 528 2700
Fax: 0131 528 2890
sophie.baker@pub-enterprises.co.uk

Select Appointments plc
Recruitment consultancy
Regent Court, Laporte Way
Beds LU4 8SB
www.select.co.uk
Contact: Debbie Smith
Tel: 01582 811600
Fax: 01582 811611
franchise@select.co.uk

ServiceMaster
Cleaning and restoration services
Tigers Road
Wigston, Leics LE18 4WS
Contact: Ken Dennis
Tel: 0116 275 9000
Fax: 0116 275 9002
kendennis@servicemaster.co.uk

Sevenoaks Sound & Vision
Electrical retail
109–113 London Road
Sevenoaks, Kent TN13 1BH
Tel: 01732 466215
www.sevenoaksfranchising.co.uk
Contact: Malcolm Blockley
Tel: 01494 431290
Fax: 01732 743981
m.blockley@btconnect.com

Signs Express
Sign makers
The Old Church, St Matthews Road
Norwich NR1 1SP
www.signsexpress.co.uk
Contact: Mr D Corbett
Tel: 01603 625925
fran@signsexpress.co.uk

Snack in the Box
Snack delivery
Dunbeath Lodge, 3 Eastern Road
Havant, Hants PO9 2JE
Contact: Mr J Lynham
Tel: 02392 799023
info@snackinthebox.freeserve.co.uk

Snack in the Box Vending Services
Snack delivery
Dunbeath Lodge, 3 Eastern Road
Havant, Hants PO9 2JE
Contact: William Owen
Tel: 0239 279 9023
Fax: 0239 279 9025
info@snackinthebox.freeserve.co.uk

Snap-on-Tools
Distribution of automotive hand tools
Telford Way
Kettering, Northants NN16 8SN
www.snapon.com
Contact: Mr Seán Derrig
Tel: 01536 413800
Fax: 01536 413900
ukweb@snapon.com

Snappy Snaps Franchises
Film processing
Glenthorne Mews, Glenthorne Road
Hammersmith, London W6 OLJ
Contact: Mr T MacAndrews
Tel: 020 8741 7474
info@snappysnaps.co.uk

Spud U Like Ltd
Fast food
9 Central Business Centre,
Great Central Way
London NW10 0UR
Contact: Mr T Schleisinger
Tel: 0181 830 2424
headoffice@spudulike.com

Stagecoach Theatre Arts
Children's theatre schools
The Courthouse, Elm Grove
Walton-on-Thames, Surrey KT12 1LZ
www.stagecoach.co.uk
Contact: Mr Manzoor Ishani
Tel: 01932 254333
Fax: 01932 256227
mail@stagecoach.co.uk

Stainbusters
Carpet and upholstery cleaning
15 Windmill Avenue,
Woolpit Business Park
Woolpit
Bury St Edmunds, Suffolk IP30 9UP
www.stainbusters.co.uk
Contact: Ms E Edwards
Tel: 01359 243800
franchise@stainbusters.co.uk

Subway
Fast food
3 Market Place
Carrickfergus, County Antrim
N Ireland BT38 7AW
www.subway.co.uk/opportunity.htm
Contact: Paul Heyes
Tel: 0800 0855058 (UK), 0044 2893 359 080 (Eire)

Fax: 02893 359102
sharp.pencil@dnet.co.uk

Swisher
Commercial hygiene
9 Churchill Court,
33 Palmerston Road
Bournemouth BH1 4HN
www.swisher.co.uk
Contact: Marilyn Keen
Tel: 01202 303333
Fax: 01202 303232
franchise@swisher.co.uk

TaxAssist Direct
Tax and accountancy
TaxAssist House,
112–114 Thorpe Road
Norwich NR1 1RT
Tel: 01603 611811
Fax: 01603 619992
www.taxassist.co.uk/franchise
Contact: Hannah Westgarth
Tel: 01603 447410
Fax: 01603 619992
hannah@taxassist.co.uk

Techclean
Cleaning of computer equipment
VDU House, Old Kiln Lane
Churt, Farnham GU10 2JH
Tel: 01428 713713
Fax: 01428 713798
Contact: Nick Zarach
Tel: 01428 713713
Fax: 01428 713798
info@techclean.co.uk

Thorntons
Chocolate and sugar confectionery
Thornton Park, Somercotes
Derby DE55 4XJ
Contact: Fiona Radford
Tel: 01773 542454
franchise@thorntons.co.uk

Toni & Guy
Hairdressing
Innovia House, Marish Wharf
St Mary's Road, Langley SL3 6DA
Contact: John Murphy
Tel: 01753 612 040
Fax: 01753 612 051
clarissa@mascolo.co.uk

Travail Employment Group
Employment agency
24 Southgate Street
Gloucester GL1 2DP
www.travail.co.uk
Contact: Bill Hendrie
Tel: 01452 420700
franchise@travail.co.uk

Tumble Tots
Pre-school playgroups
Bluebird Park, Bromsgrove Road
Hunnington, Halesowen, W Mids
B62 0TT
www.tumbletots.com
Contact: David Hunt
Tel: 0121 585 7003
Fax: 0121 585 6891
david.hunt@tumbletots.com

Unigate Dairies
Distribution of milk and dairy products
14/40 Victoria Road
Aldershot, Hants GU1 1TH
www.unigate.plc.uk
Contact: Mr H Allam
Tel: 01252 366966
hugh.allam@dairycrest.co.uk

Urban Planters
Indoor plants
202 Pasture Lane
Bradford, W Yorks BD7 2SE
www.urbanplanters.co.uk
Contact: Mr N Gresty
Tel: 01274 579331
may@urbanplanters.co.uk

Vendo
Commercial vehicle power washing
215 East Lane
Wembley, Mddx HA0 3NG
Contact: Mr I Calhoun
Tel: 0208 908 1234

Ventrolla
Window renovation
11 Hornbeam Square South
South Harrogate, N Yorks HG2 8NB
Tel: 01423 870011
www.ventrolla.co.uk
Contact: Mr S C Emmerson
Tel: 01423 859323
Fax: 01423 859321
info@ventrolla.co.uk

Viewplus
Home delivery of entertainment for rental
The Forum, 277 London Road
Burgess Hill, W Sussex RH15 9QU
Tel: 01444 240250
Fax: 01444 240251
Contact: Helen Monteiro
sales@viewplus.co.uk

The Village Green Team
Home and lifestyle maintenance
Burrough Court, Burrough on the Hill
Melton Mowbray, Leics LE14 2QS
Contact: Colleen Denby
Tel: 01664 454700
info@villagegreenteam.com

Vision Express
Retail opticians
Abbeyfield Road
Lenton, Nottingham NG7 2SP
Contact: Simon Innes
Tel: 01159 882013
Fax: 01159 882380
lyn.sawyer@visionexpress.com

Wimpy International
Fast food
2 The Listons, Liston Road
Marlow, Bucks SL7 1FD
www.wimpyburgers.co.uk
Contact: Brian Crambac
Tel: 01628 891655
mailroom@wimpy-restaurants.com

Associate members

These are companies with a growing franchise network and evidence of successful franchising for a period of one year with at least one franchisee. To become an Associate Member of the BFA, franchisors are required to submit a completed application form, including disclosure document, franchise agreement, prospectus and accounts, and provide proof of a correctly constituted pilot scheme successfully operated for at least one year, financed and managed by the applicant company (as for Full Membership) but with evidence of successful franchising for a period of one year with at least one franchisee.

Agency Express
Estate agency board contractors
The Old Church, St Matthews Road
Norwich NK1 1SP
Contact: Stephen Watson
Tel: 01603 620044
Fax: 01603 613136
agency.express@btinternet.com

Alliance Preservation
Building preservation services
Nothgate House, St Marys Place
Newcastle upon Tyne NE1 7PN
Tel: 0800 096 9390
www.alliance-preservation.com
Contact: William Kidd
Tel: 0800 096 9390
tyrer.kidd@virgin.net

AWG Windscreens
Replacement and repair of windscreens
Unit 4, Sheppards Business Park
Norwich Road, Lenwade
Norwich NR9 5SH
www.awgwindscreens.com
Contact: Mr P Giles
Tel: 01603 870999

Fax: 01603 871387
info@awgwindscreens.com

Barrett & Coe
Training in wedding and portrait photography
79A Thorpe Road
Norwich, Norfolk NR1 1UA
www.barrettandcoe.co.uk
Contact: Andrew Coe
Tel: 01603 629739
enquire@barrettandcoe.co.uk

Benjys
Mobile catering
5th Floor, 33 Cornhill
London EC3V 3ND
Tel: 020 7626 2502
Fax: 020 7626 2503
Contact: Andrew Quail
Tel: 0207 626 2502
Fax: 0207 626 2503
franchise@benjys-sandwiches.com

Capelli
Distribution of hair salon products
Park House, South Street
Farnham, Surrey GU9 7QQ
Tel: 01252 892 350
Fax: 01252 892 351
www.capellisp.com
Contact: Carl Atkinson
Tel: 01252 892350
Fax: 01252 892351
mail@capellisp.com

Cartridge World
Refill printer cartridges
Unit A3, Hornbeam Square West
Hornbeam Park
Harrogate, N Yorks HG2 8PA
Contact: Duncan Berry
Tel: 01423 878520
Fax: 01423 878521
duncan@cartridgeworld.org

Chips Franchise
New and refurbished video games, consoles and accessories
63–65 Borough Road
Middlesbrough TS1 3AA
Tel: 0870 0130 028
Fax: 01642 351477
www.chipsworld.co.uk
Contact: Debra McCabe
Tel: 0870 0130 028
Fax: 01642 351477
franchise@chipsworld.co.uk

CNA International
Executive Recruitment
4 Boundary Court,
Willow Farm Business Park
Castle Donington, Derby DE74 2UD
Tel: 01332 856200
Fax: 01332 856222
www.cnainternational.co.uk
Contact: Paula Reed
Tel: 01332 856200
Fax: 01332 856222
info@cnainternational.co.uk

Countrywide Assured Franchising
Property services
Century House, Rosemount Avenue
West Byfleet, Surrey KT14 6LB
Tel: 01932 350314
www.cafl.co.uk
Contact: Alan Snowball
Tel: 01932 350314
Fax: 01932 350587
enquiries@cafl.co.uk

Countrywide Signs Limited
Estate agency board suppliers and contractors
105 Wyberton West Road
Boston, Lincs PE21 7JU
Tel: 01205 363909
Fax: 01205 364640
www.countrywide-signs.com
Contact: Martin Baker
Tel: 01205 363909
Fax: 01205 364640
operations@countrywide-signs.com

Dancia International
Retail dancewear
8 Western Street
Brighton BN1 2PG
www.dancia.co.uk/franchise
Contact: Mr T Kirkup
Tel: 0800 5423262
dancia@lineone.net

Davis Coleman
Banking and legal agents
PO Box 5498
Ongar, Essex CM5 0TJ
Contact: Harry Varney
Tel: 01277 364333
Fax: 01277 364773
h.varney@daviscoleman.com

Dream Doors
Kitchen refurbishment and fitting
16 Stoke Road
Gosport, Hants PO12 1JB
Contact: Troy Tappenden
Tel: 02392 361295
Fax: 02392 346428
dreamdoorsltd@tiscali.co.uk

Eismann International
Home delivery of frozen foods
Margarethe House, Eismann Way
Phoenix Park Ind Estate
Corby NN17 1ZB
Contact: Mr K Schneider
Tel: 01536 275100
Fax: 01538 275106
cmgivern@eismann.co.uk

Expense Reduction Analysts
Cost management services
St Paul, Cross Street
Winchester, Hants SO23 8SZ
www.era-auditel.net
Contact: Robert Allison
Tel: 01962 849444
kate@era-auditel.net

Express Despatch
Parcel distribution
Unit 4, Fairview Industrial Estate
Kingsbury Road
Crudworth B76 9EE
Contact: Louis John
Tel: 01675 475757
admin@hq.expressdespatch.co.uk

Fastsigns
Signage
Fastsigns International,
2550 Midway Rd
Suite 150
Carrollton TX 75006 2372, USA
Tel: 0800 093 4977
Contact: Jenny Boreham
jenny.boreham@fastsigns.com

Filta Group
Purification of cooking oils
The Locks, Hillmorton
Rugby CV21 4PP
Contact: Mr V Clewes
Tel: 01788 550100
Fax: 01788 551839
enquiries@filtagroup.com

Finning Hydraulic Services
Hydraulic hose replacement
Watling Street
Cannock, Staffs WS11 3LL
www.finning.co.uk/fhs
Contact: Alan Gibson
Tel: 01543 461654
Fax: 01543 461737
aludlow@finning.co.uk

Flowers Forever
Preservation of wedding bouquets
Sterling House,
10G Buntsford Park Road
Bromsgrove, Worcs B60 3DX
Tel: 01527 880 200
Fax: 01527 880 201
Contact: Fiona Williams
Tel: 01527 880 200
Fax: 01527 880 201
info@flowersforever.co.uk

Franchise Development Services
Franchise consultancy
Franchise House, 56 Surrey Street
Norwich NR1 3FD
www.franchise-group.com
Contact: Roy Seaman
Tel: 01603 620301
Fax: 01603 630174
enquiries@fdsltd.com

Granite Transformations
Kitchen worktop resurfacing
Unit 5, Tunbridge Wells Trade
Longfield Road
Tunbridge Wells TN2 3QF
www.granitetransformations.com
Contact: Bill Croney
Tel: 07775 508227
bill@granite-transformations.co.uk

Green Cleen
Wheeled bin washing
18 Ladforfields Industrial Park
Seighford, Staffs ST18 9QE
Contact: Marius Coulon
Tel: 01785 282855
Fax: 01785 281300
sales@greencleen.com

Greenthumb
Domestic lawn treatment service
Third Avenue, Deeside Industrial Park
Deeside, Flintshire CH5 2LA
Contact: Stephen Waring
Tel: 01244 287955
Fax: 01244 287956
franchise@greenthumb.co.uk

Helen O'Grady Children's Drama Academy
Children's Theatre Training
North Side
Vale, Guernsey GY3 5TX
Tel: 01481 200250
Fax: 01481 200247
Contact: Mr N Le Page
Tel: 01481 200250
Fax: 01481 200247
helenogrady@cwgsy.net

Hydro-Dynamix
Industrial cleaning
Greenwich House, Peel Street
Maidstone, Kent ME14 2BP
Contact: James Every
Tel: 01622 664993
Fax: 01662 695170
james.every@hydro-dynamix.com

Jani King
Contract cleaning
150 London Road
Kingston upon Thames, Surrey
KT2 6QL
Contact: Mr P Howarth
Tel: 0208 481 4300
Fax: 0208 481 4343
julied862@janikinggb.co.uk

Kids Klub
Children's entertainment videos
Klub House, Downside
Salisbury SP3 5PH
www.kids-klub.co.uk
Contact: Mr G Thomas
Tel: 01747 871004
Fax: 01747 870414
info@kids-klub.co.uk

King Acre Landscaping Centre
Retail landscape
Bowland Stone, Crews Hole Road
St George, Bristol BS5 8AU
Contact: Karen Lowden
Tel: 0117 955 130
Fax: 01252 404 559
kingacre@bowlandbristol.com

La Baguette Du Jour
Sandwich cafe and espresso bar
F18 Ashmount Business Park
Upper Forest Way,
Swansea Enterprise Park
Swansea SA6 8QR
Contact: Mark Meadon
Tel: 01792 790701
Fax: 01792 791006
hq@bag-du-jour.freeserve.co.uk

Leadership Management
Management training
18 Bells Hill Green
Stoke Poges, Bucks SL2 4BY UK
Tel: 01753 669358
Fax: 01753 669458
www.lmi-ukfranchise.com
Contact: Mrs T Coutts
Tel: 01753 669358
Fax: 01753 669458
jointheteam@lmi-uk.com

Mail Boxes Etc
Business, postal & communications services
Unit 9, The Alfold Business Centre
Loxwood Road, Surrey GU6 8HP
www.mbe.uk.com
Contact: Mr Chris Gilliam
Tel: 01403 759300
Fax: 01403 753820
cgilliam@mbe.co.uk

Mitchells and Butlers Business Franchise
Pub Retail
27 Fleet Street
Birmingham B3 1JP
Contact: Simon Higginbottom
Tel: 0121 4984463
Fax: 0121 2332246
simon.higginbottom@mbplc.com

Money Shop
Cheque cashing financial services
Castlebridge Office Village
Kirtley Drive, Castle Marina
Nottingham NG7 1LD
Tel: 01244 505505
Contact: Courtney Vaughan
Tel: 01244 505505
Fax: 01244 505509
marie.roberts@dfg.com

Monkey Music
Music and singing classes for pre-school children
Unit 3, Thrales End Farm
Thrales End Lane
Harpenden AL5 3NS
www.monkeymusic.co.uk
Contact: Angie Davies
Tel: 01582 469242
Fax: 01582 469600
jointheteam@monkeymusic.co.uk

Muffin Break
Café/bakery
Allways House, Castle Street
Cambridge CB3 0DU
Contact: Mike Arbuckle
Tel: 01223 308781
Fax: 01223 308782
mike@muffinbreak.co.uk

NIC Franchising
Contract cleaning
Hoyland House, Forge Lane
Leeds LS12 2HG
Contact: John Pinnick
Tel: 0113 2310210
mob 07730 922472
Fax: 0113 2310669
jpinnick@nicgroup.co.uk

Nippers
Retail nursery goods and toys
21 Mount Ephraim Road
Tunbridge Wells, Kent TN1 1EN
www.nippers.co.uk
Contact: Mrs J Cassel
Tel: 01892 516 617
Fax: 01892 516 500
nippers@which.net

No Graffiti
Graffiti removal and protection
15 Windmill Avenue, Woolpit
Business Park
Woolpit, Suffolk IP30 9UP
Contact: Richard Edwards
Tel: 01359 243802
Fax: 01359 243808
lesley.cooper@nograffiti.co.uk

Northwood Residential Lettings
1 Bellevue Road
Southampton SO15 2AW
Tel: 02380 336677
Fax: 02380 333789
www.northwoodfranchises.co.uk
Contact: Andrew Goodson
Tel: 02380 336677
Fax: 02380 333789
sales@northwoodfranchises.co.uk

Oscar Pet Foods
Pet food home delivery
Bannister Hall Mill, Higher Walton
Preston, Lancs PR5 4DB
Contact: Mr M Dancy
Tel: 01772 647900
discover@oscars.co.uk

Pentagon Glass Tech
Window tinting for cars
Pentagon House
Unit 4, Acton Park Estate
The Vale, London W3 7QE
Contact: Geoff Russell
Tel: 0208 7499749
Fax: 0208 7494499
craigs@pentagonglasstech.com

Planet Franchising
Retail conservatories, windows and doors
5 Peregrine Place
Moss Side, Leyland, Lancs PR25 3EY
Contact: Mr J Reddecliffe
Tel: 01772 452225
Fax: 01772 452226
jos@planetpvc.co.uk

The Power Service
Gas & electrical safety inspection
Units 5 & 6, Reliant House
Oakmere Mews, Oakmere Lane
Potters Bar EN6 5DT
Contact: Stephen Begg
Tel: 01707 654600
Fax: 01707 647119
franchise@the-power-service.co.uk

Prestige Nursing
Health care recruitment
1st Floor, Leo House
Railway Approach, Wallington SM6 0JJ

Contact: Jonathan Bruce
Tel: 0208 254 7500
Fax: 0208 773 3525
k.sharpe@prestige-nursing.co.uk

Profit Focus Group
Management consulting
Polysec House,
Blackpole Trading Estate
Hindlip Lane, Worcester WR3 8TJ
Contact: Phil Guest
Tel: 01905 342000
Fax: 01905 455588
philguest@profitfocus.net

Puccino's
Speciality coffee bars
Unit 6, First Quarter
Longmead Business Park
Epsom, Surrey KT19 9XX
Tel: 01372 74411
Fax: 01372 741155
Contact: Mr Bassem Beckdache
Tel: 01372 744411
Fax: 01372 741155
bassemb@puccinos.co.uk

Re-Nu
Replacement kitchen & bedrooms
60 Nuffield Road
Nuffield Industrial Estate
Poole, Dorset BH17 0RS
Contact: Meryl Ponsford
Tel: 01202 687642
merylponsford@re-nu.fsnet.co.uk

Salon Services
Hair and beauty supplies
82 Kelvin Avenue, Hillington
Industrial Estate
Glasgow G52 4LT

Contact: Ms M Burns
Tel: 0141 882 3355
franchising@salon-services.co.uk

Scenic Blue
Landscape gardening
The Plant Centre, Brogdale
Brogdale Road
Faversham, Kent ME13 8XZ
www.scenicblue.co.uk
Contact: Tony Mundella
Tel: 0800 783 3428
Fax: 01795 591059
mail@scenicblue.co.uk

Sign a Rama
Sign makers
7 Herald Business Park,
Golden Acres Lane
Coventry CV3 2SY
Contact: Martyn Ward
Tel: 02476 659933
Fax: 02476 659944
signinfo@signarama.com

Sliderobes
Bedroom furniture with sliding doors
Sliderobes House,
61 Boucher Crescent
Belfast BT12 6HU
Tel: 028 9068 1034
Fax: 028 9066 1032
www.sliderobes.com
Contact: Alan Brown
Tel: 028 90 681034
Fax: 028 90 661032
alan.brown@sliderobes.com

Stumpbusters
Tree stump grinding specialists
Hill House, Brimmers Road
Princes Risborough, Bucks HP27 0LE
Contact: Mr A Broom
Tel: 01844 342851
stump@globalnet.co.uk

Trophy Pet Foods
Mobile pet food
11–12 Market Place
Faringdon, Oxon SN7 7HP
Contact: Sue Reid
Tel: 01367 243434
Fax: 01367 243737
sales@trophypetfoods.co.uk

UNIGLOBE
Business and leisure travel agencies
120 Wilton Road
London SW1V 1JZ
www.uniglobetravel.co.uk
Contact: Phil Pinkney
Tel: 01252 810792
Fax: 01252 810792
ppinkney@uniglobetravel.co.uk

Venture Portraits
Portrait photographers
Premier Park, Road One
Winsford, Cheshire CW7 3PT
Contact: Jonathan Cullen
Tel: 01606 558854
Fax: 01606 559203
jackie@ventureportraits.com

The Wheelie Bin Cleaning Company
Cleaning of wheeled refuse bins
Mwyndy Cross, Mwyndy
Pontyclun, Mid Glamorgan
CF72 8PN
www.wheeliebin.com
Contact: Kevyn Lloyd
Tel: 01443 237800
Fax: 01443 229000
info@wheeliebin.com

White Knight Laundry Services
72 George Street
Caversham, Reading, Berks
RG4 8DW
Contact: Robert Adams
Tel: 01189 462233
robertadams@white-knight.co.uk

Provisional members

These are companies new to franchising, developing their franchise concept, and taking BFA accredited advice on its structure.

247Staff
Recruitment
Granby Chambers, 1 Halford Street
Leicester LE1 1JA
www.247staff.net/franchise
Contact: The franchise team
Tel: 0845 225 5025
Fax: 07043 301684
info@247staff.net

Antal International Network
Executive recruitment
Regent House, 24–25 Nutford Place
London W1H 5YN
www.antalfranchising.com
Contact: Kevin Cox
Tel: 0870 7745464
Fax: 0870 7745465
franchise@antal.com

Autoshine Express
Vehicle wash and car care
Whitburn Road
Birniehill, Bathgate
West Lothian EH48 2HR
www.autoshine-express.co.uk
Contact: James Allison
Tel: 01506 650590
Fax: 01506 650393
franchising@autoshine-express.co.uk

Bark Busters
Home dog training
Highfields House
Worleston, Cheshire CW5 6DU
www.barkbusters.co.uk
Contact: Tony O'Herlihy
Tel: 01270 522456
Fax: 01270 522 106
info@barkbusters.co.uk

Barking Mad Ltd
Home-from-home pet care
Knights Errant, Church Lane
Tunstall, Lancs LA6 2RP
Tel: 015242 73301
Contact: Mrs Lee Southern
Tel: 015242 73301
leesouthern@barkingmad.uk.com

Bartercard UK
Trade exchange
Bartercard House, Brooklands Close
Sunbury, Mddx TW16 7DY
www.bartercard.co.uk
Contact: Alun Hamilton-Jervis
Tel: 01932 772772
Fax: 0870 751 8512
alun.hamilton-
jervis@uk.bartercard.com

Bin Masters
Van-based repair of waste containers
Suite 1, Elm House, Shackleford Road
Elstead, Surrey GU8 6LB
Tel: 01252 703 429
www.binmasters.co.uk
Contact: Roy Gratton
Tel: 01252 703 429
royg@binmasters.co.uk

Chameleon NCF
Telecommunications installation
Brunel Way, Severalls Business Park
Colchester, Essex CO4 4QX
Contact: Mrs Ali Hysom
Tel: 01206 500863
Fax: 01206 500852
ahysom@thechameleongroup.co.uk

Chancellors Executive Search
Chancellor House
11 Park Road
St Annes on Sea, Lancs FY8 1PW
Contact: Stephen Breeze
Tel: 0870 8702382
Fax: 01253 789913
ces@chancellors-recruitment.co.uk

ChipsAway International
Vehicle paint repair
ChipsAway House, Arthur Drive
Hoo Farm Trading Estate
Kidderminster, Worcs DY11 7RA
Contact: Nick Bicknell
Tel: 0800 7316914
uk@chipsaway.co.uk

Clive's Easylearn Pop Music Schools
Music tuition
3–7 Thornhill Park Rd
Southampton SO18 5TP
www.clivesmusic.com
Contact: Clive Brooks
Tel: 02380 477433
franchise@clivesmusic.com

Concept Solutions
Insurance claims
4 The Printworks, Hey Road
Clitheroe BB7 9WA
Tel: 01254 825 250

Fax: 01254 825 251
Contact: James Whittle
Tel: 01254 825250
Fax: 01254 825251
franchise@concept-claims.co.uk

Connect 2
Promotional merchandise
17 Charnwood Fields
Sutton Bonington, Loughborough
LE12 5NP
Contact: Malcolm Dade
Tel: 01509 673179
Fax: 01509 673828
sales@connect2first.com

Cotton Bottoms
Nappy laundry
7–9 Water Lane Ind Est, Water Lane
Storrington, W Sussex RH20 3XX
Contact: Joanne Freer
Tel: 0870 777 8899
Fax: 0870 777 8700
sales@cottonbottoms.co.uk

Crepe A Croissant
Crepe and sandwich bar
50 Enoch Square
Glasgow G1 4DH
Contact: Mr K Nahar
Tel: 0800 316 9333
Fax: 0141 248 7114
info@crepeacroissant.co.uk

Devonshire Art Publishers
Greeting cards distribution
7 Park Royal Metro Centre
Britannia Way, Coronation Road
London NW10 7PA
Contact: Marcella Rowan
Tel: 020 8691 6611

Fax: 020 8691 9169
devonshirecards@btinternet.com

The Drive Doctor
Driveway restoration
Bamber Lodge, Newton Road
Lowton WA3 1NU
Contact: Michael Palin
Tel: 0800 169 4469
info@drivedoctor.uk.com

Driver Transport Training
Unit 2, Shepherds Grove Industrial Estate East
Stanton, Bury St Edmunds IP31 2BG
Contact: Brian Hewitt
Tel: 01359 251717
Fax: 01359 253601
brian@d-t-t.co.uk

DRL
Fire and flood restoration
2 Lex Building, Cranes Close
Basidon, Essex SS14 3JD
Tel: 01268 595219
Fax: 01268 521298
Contact: Franchise manager
Tel: 01268 595219
Fax: 01268 521298
franchiseinfo@drl.net

ERA Great Britain
Estate agency
Colchester Business Centre,
1 George William Way
Colchester CO1 2JS
Contact: Lorraine Aldridge
Tel: 01206 713650
Fax: 01206 713669
roygover@eragb.co.uk

ExChina Franchising
Imports and exports
East Midlands Airport Office
Herald Way, Pegasus Business Park
Castle Donnington DE47 2TZ
www.franchisechina.co.uk
Contact: The franchise team
Tel: 0845 22 55 800
mail@franchisechina.co.uk

Furniture Pro
Furniture repair
Valspar Industries Ltd,
152 Milton Park
Abingdon, Oxon OX14 4SD
Contact: Craig Henthorn
Tel: 01235 444749
Fax: 01235 862730
chenthorn@valspar.com

Gas-Elec Safety Systems
Safety inspection
Brooklyn House, Money Lane
The Green, West Drayton UB7 7PQ
Contact: Carol Otway
Tel: 01895 420777
carol.otway@gas-elec.co.uk

Globalink International
Telecommunications
Globalink House, Honeybridge Lane
Dial Post, Horsham, W Sussex
RH13 8NX
Contact: Phil Gaffer
Tel: 0870 8455655
Fax: 0870 8455656
sales@globalinkgroup.com

Go Cruise
Sale of cruises
80 Hewell Road, Barnt Green
Birmingham B45 8NF
Tel: 0121 445 7211
www.cruisefranchise.co.uk
Contact: Clive Howard
Tel: 0121 445 7211
Fax: 0870 9908824
charlesw@gocruisedirect.co.uk

Hair on Broadway
Hairdressing
333 Watling Street
Radlett, Herts WD7 7LB
Contact: David Twyman
Tel: 01923 854100
Fax: 01923 850565
hob@btconnect.com

Hot Bite
Hot food vending
Southwood Farm, Southwood Road
Shalden, Alton, Hants GU34 4EB
Tel: 01420 80230
Fax: 01420 87562
Contact: Nigel Lennard
Tel: 01420 80230
Fax: 01420 87562
enquiries@hotbite.co.uk

House Doctor
Interior design
Balgonie House, Acer Cries
Paisley PA2 9LN
Contact: Doreen Smith
Tel: 0141 8842319
Fax: 0141 8847802
info@housedoctoruk.com

Hudson's Coffee House
Gourmet coffee and food
122–124 Colmore Row
Birmingham B3 3AU
Tel: 01837 851363
Fax: 01837 851549
Contact: Iain Martin
Tel: 08701 044 233
Fax: 08701 044 234
igm@kyros.uk.com

Icon Business Solutions
Business consultancy
Parkshot House, 5 Kew Road
Richmond, Surrey TW9 2PR
Contact: Nardia Booshand
Tel: 020 8334 8043
Fax: 020 8334 8100
infouk@iconbusinesssolutions.com

Ideal Handling
Health and safety products and services
1 Globe Chambers, 76 High Street
Uppermill, Oldham OL3 6AW
Contact: Mr Thornton
Tel: 01457 810022
Fax: 01457 810033
andy@ideal-handling.com

The Independent Mortgage Advice Bureau
Mortgage Advice
139 The Parade
Watford, Herts WD1 1NA
Contact: Russell Sanders
Tel: 01727 893696
Fax: 01727 893499
russell.sanders@imab.net

Ink Xpress
Refilling inkjet cartridges
4 Alpha Business Park,
Whitehouse Road
Ipswich IP1 5LT
Contact: Nicholas Reid
Tel: 01473 242720

IPWFI Franchising
Insurance for the double glazing and building industry
Apex House,
172 Blackmoorfoot Road
Crosland Moor
Huddersfield, W Yorks HD4 5RE
Contact: John Heward
Tel: 01484 303900
Fax: 01484 462463
ipwfi@aol.com

Just Lets Property Management
Property Management
142 Oundle Road
Woodston, Peterborough PE2 9PJ
Contact: Miss Steph Heron
Tel: 01832 275158
Fax: 01832 275159
franchise@justlets.com

Lasertech
Distribution of printer consumables
Wharfside Ind. Estate, Wharf Street
Howley, Warrington WA1 2HT
Contact: Mr J Williams
Tel: 01925 23 23 23
Fax: 01925 23 07 08
franchise@lasertech.co.uk

Lincary Recruitment
Victoria Chambers, 63 High Street
Barnstaple EX31 1JB
Contact: Karen Lambert
Tel: 0871 222 1926
Fax: 01271 379927
www.lincary.co.uk
admin@lincary.co.uk

The Little Gym
Physical fitness for children
Mindful Development,
Compass House
Riverside West, Smugglers Way
London SW18 1DB
Contact: Alexander De Wit
Tel: +32 10 23 17 90
Fax: +32 10 88 16 65

Little Impressions
Plaster cast momentos
7 Bulkington Avenue
Worthing, Sussex BN14 7HH
Contact: Mrs F North
Tel: 01903 230515
Fax: 01903 603120
info@little-impressions.com

Mobile Car Valeting
Car Valeting
The Barn, 211A Swithland Lane
Ruthley, Leicester
Contact: Mr T Smith
Tel: 0116 2303040
terry@mobilecarvaleting.co.uk

Monk Marketing
Promotional merchandise
63a Brighton Road
Shoreham by Sea, W Sussex
BN43 6RE
Contact: Michael Monk
Tel: 01273 464010
Fax: 01273 464131
enquiries@monkmarketing.com

Mr Bagels Franchise
Catering and hotels
87 Reighton Road
Upper Clapton, London E5 8SQ
Contact: Mr Avi Kahlani
Tel: 020 88064445
Fax: 020 8067502
mrbagels2000@msn.com

Netspace
Internet products and services
John Eccles House,
Robert Robinson Avenue
Oxford OX4 4GP
Tel: 0870 770 2545
Fax: 0870 770 2546
Contact: Shaun Thomson
shaun@netspace-uk.co.uk

Oakleaf Sales
Interior decoration
Lingbob Mills, Main Street
Wilsden, W Yorks BD15 0JP
Tel: 01535 272878
Contact: Jonathan Banister
Tel: 01535 272 878
Fax: 01535 275 748
jon@oakleaf.co.uk

Onepointfor
Convenience retailer
The Centre for Advanced Industry
Coble Dene, Royal Quays
North Shields NE29 6DE
Tel: 0191 296 3206
Fax: 0191 296 3142
Contact: Amy O'Neill
enquiries@onepointfor.com

Petpals UK
Pet care
Basepoint Business and Innovation Centre
Caxton Close, East Portway
Andover, Hants SP10 3FG
www.petpals.com
Contact: Tracey Eden
Tel: 01264 326362
Fax: 01264 326361
franchise@petpals.com

Pierre Lang
Designer jewellery
Peter Southgate, PO Box 3324
Wokingham, Berks RG41 5QV
www.pierrelang.co.uk
Contact: Pierre Lang
Tel: 0118 9782851
Fax: 0118 9782876
plang777aol.com

Pinnacle Chauffeur Transport
Luxury chauffeur
Unit 5, Crown Business Centre
George Street
Failsworth, Manchester M35 9BW
Contact: Mr Chris Brown
Tel: 0161 6821118
Fax: 0161 6821135
Chrisbrown@wedriveyou.co.uk

Pizza Hut
Pizza delivery and take away
1 Imperial Place, Elstree Way
Borehamwood, Herts WD6 1JN
Tel: 0208 2327900
Fax: 0208 2329001
reception@tdatransitions.co.uk

PPS Franchising
Recruitment management
Centre Court, 1301 Stratford Road
Birmingham B28 9HH
Contact: Alan Ross
Tel: 0121 7772332
Fax: 0121 7786638
birmingham@pps500.co.uk

Prewer and Orsborn
Lighting retail and consultancy
Unit 2, Hockliffe Business Park
Hockcliffe LU7 9NB
Contact: Warren Prewer
Tel: 01252 211511
Fax: 01252 211183
warren@prewer-orsborn.co.uk

Printing.com
Print design and supply
Focal Point, 3rd Avenue, The Village
Trafford Park, Manchester M17 1FG
Contact: Alan Roberts
Tel: 0161 848 5713
alan.roberts@printing.com

Protex Solutions
Tyre sealant
Solutions House
Bessemer Close,
Ebblake Industrial Estate
Verwood, Dorset BH31 6AZ
Contact: Barry Watkins
Tel: 01202 810000
Fax: 01202 810001

Punctureseal International
Tyre sealant
St Brandons House,
29 Great George Street
Bristol BS1 5QT
Contact: Spiro Ginis
Tel: 0117 9200047
Fax: 0117 9200001

Regus Franchise International
Business centres
3000 Hillswood Drive
Chertsey, Surrey KT16 0RS
Contact: Mr R Arman
Tel: 01932 895194
Fax: 01932 895001
richard.arman@regus.com

Riverford Organic Vegetables
Home delivery of organic vegetable boxes
Wash Barn
Buckfastleigh, Devon TQ11 0LD
www.riverford.co.uk
Contact: Mr M Swarbrick
Tel: 01803 762720
Fax: 01803 762718
franchise@riverford.co.uk

The Sales Recruitment Network
Specialist Recruitment
1–2 North End
Swineshead, Boston, Lincs PE20 3LR
www.tsrn.co.uk
Contact: Richard Langrick
Tel: 0870 350 1071
Fax: 0870 350 1072
info@tsrn.co.uk

Smart Cartridge
Refilling office machine cartridges
Unit 1, Swanston Steading
109 Swanston Road
Edinburgh EH10 7DS
Contact: Miss S Lampshire
Tel: 0131 445 7607
Fax: 0131 445 7608
slampshire@smart-cartridge.com

Smiffy's
Party shops
R H Smith and Son, Peckett Plaza
Heapham Road South
Gainsborough, Lincs
Contact: Richard Pickworth
Tel: 01427 616831
Fax: 01427 619718
helenrushworth@smiffys.com

Sound Steps
Children's keyboard/piano lessons
Acorn House,
74/94 Cherry Orchard Road
Croydon CR9 6DA
www.soundstepsmusic.co.uk
Contact: Nigel Blyth
Tel: 0208 688 1147
Fax: 0208 680 1996
info@soundstepsmusic.co.uk

Steamatic
Carpet and air duct cleaning
303 Arthur Street
Fort Worth, TX 76107, USA
Contact: Mr B Sims
Tel: 817 332 1575
bsims@steamatic.com

Success Photography
Moleside, 9 Reigate Road
Sidlow Reigate, Surrey RH2 8QH
Contact: Kate Bell
Tel: 01293 822211
Fax: 01293 820642
kate@successphotography.com

Sumo
Underground utilities detection
PO Box 522, Caslon Court
Pitronerie Road
St Peter Port, Guernsey GY1 2RW
Contact: Colin Carnachan
Tel: 01481 713425
Fax: 01481 729554
website@sumoservices.com

Superseal International
Puncture protection
30 Derrylettiff Road
Portadown, Co Armagh BT62 IQU
Contact: Mr M Lavery
Tel: 0870 744 3750
info@puncturepross.com

Sureslim
Retail sale of eating programmes
23–25 Bell Street
Reigate, Surrey RH2 7AD
Tel: 0870 321 4014
Fax: 0870 321 4015
Contact: Mr A Styant
Tel: 01737 229761
Fax: 01737 229769
alan@sureslimuk.com

Surface Doctor
Resurfacing of bathrooms and kitchens
Unit D12, Hortonwood 7
Telford, Salop TF1 7GP
Contact: Mr Roger Plantier
Tel: 0870 444 8250
Fax: 0870 444 8251
www.surfacedoctor.co.uk
rplantier@surfacedoctor.co.uk

Survair Franchising
Protective coatings for property
Caolila
Glendevon FK14 7JY, Scotland
Contact: Damian McConnell
Tel: 01259 781282
Fax: 01259 781291
damian@survair-franchising.com

The Sweet Partnership
Confectionery distribution
Units 4 & 5, Metana House
Priestley Way, Crawley RH10 9NT
Contact: Paul Balfe
Tel: 01293 551599
Fax: 01293 552620
pbalfe.tsp@ukonline.co.uk

That Cafe
Internet cafe
PO Box 23545, EH3 9YR
Contact: Paul Taylor
Tel: 0870 770 4121
Fax: 0870 771 4122
www.ThatinternetCafe.net
franchising@ThatInternetCafe.net

West End Training
Training and outplacement
Temple Court, Cathedral Road
Cardiff
Contact: Clive Sherer
Tel: 029 2078 6429
Fax: 029 2078 6666
info@westendtraining.co.uk

The Wilsher Group
Management consultancy
Hartham Pack
Corsham, Wilts SN13 0RP
www.wilsher-group.com
Contact: Mike Wilsher
Tel: 01249 700250
Fax: 01249 700251
Mike.Wilsher@wilsher-group.com

The Workpoint
Recruitment company
98 Bradshaw Gate
Bolton, Lancs BL1 1QJ
Contact: Malcolm Hughes
Tel: 01204 532711
Fax: 01204 364461
bolton@temporecruitment.co.uk

Your Move
Estate agency
Your Move Franchising
Chamberlain House, Paradise Place
Birmingham B3 3HJ
Contact: Neil Knight
Tel: 0121 262 5321
Fax: 0121 262 5222
franchising@your-move.co.uk

Affiliated professional advisers

Experienced franchising advisers able to offer help and advice to both franchisors and franchisees.

Solicitors

Addleshaw Goddard
100 Barbirolli Square
Manchester M2 3AB
Contact: Mr G Lindrup
Tel: 0161 934 6255
Fax: 0181 960 9655
garth.lindrup@addleshawgoddard.com

Beachcroft Wansbroughs
St Ann's House, St Ann Street
Manchester M2 7LP
Contact: Pauline Cowie
Tel: 0161 934 3111
Fax: 0161 934 3288
pcowie@bwlaw.co.uk

Berwin Leighton Paisner
Adelaide House, London Bridge
London EC4R 9HA
Contact: Mr J Sipling
Tel: 0207 760 1000
Fax: 0207 760 1111
John.sipling@berwinleighpaisner.co.uk

Biggart Baillie & Gifford
Dalmore House,
310 St Vincent Street
Glasgow G2 5QR
Contact: Mr C Miller
Tel: 0141 228 8000
info@biggartbaillie.co.uk

Blake Lapthorn Linnell
Kings Court, 21 Brunswick Place
Southampton SO15 2AQ
www.bllaw.co.uk
Contact: Geoffrey Sturgess
Tel: 023 8063 1823
Fax: 023 8022 6294
geoffrey.sturgess@bllaw.co.uk

Brodies
15 Atholl Crescent
Edinburgh EH3 8HA
Contact: Mr J C A Voge
Tel: 0131 228 3777
julian.voge@brodies.co.uk

Chambers & Co
Jonathan Scott Hall, Thorpe Road
Norwich NR1 1UH
Contact: Mr J Chambers
Tel: 01603 616155
chambers@paston.co.uk

Clairmonts
9 Clairmont Gardens
Glasgow G3 7LW
Contact: Mr D S Kaye
Tel: 0141 3314000
info@clairmonts.co.uk

David Bigmore & Co
Thornton Grange, Chester Road
Gresford LL12 8NU
www.dbigmore.co.uk

Appendices / 175

Contact: David Bigmore
Tel: 01978 855058
Fax: 01978 854623
db@dbigmore.co.uk

Eversheds
1 Royal Standard Place
Nottingham NG1 6FZ
Contact: Mr M Knibbs
Tel: 0115 950 7000
nottingham@eversheds.com

Eversheds
Senator House,
85 Queen Victoria Street
London EC4V 4JL
Contact:
Mr M Mendelsohn or Chris Wormald
Tel: 0207 919 4862
chriswormald@eversheds.com

Eversheds
115 Colmore Row
Birmingham B3 3AL
Contact: Mr Andrew Fordham
Tel: 0121 232 1232
andrewfordham@eversheds.co.uk

Eversheds
Eversheds House, 70 Great
Bridgewater Street
Manchester M1 5ES
Contact: Ms R Connorton
Tel: 0161 831 8000
Fax: 0161 832 5337
ruthconnorton@eversheds.co.uk

Eversheds
Central Square South, Orchard Street
Newcastle upon Tyne NE1 3XX
Contact: Ms R Connorton

Tel: 0191 241 6000
Fax: 0191 241 6499
ruthconnorton@eversheds.co.uk

Eversheds
Cloth Hall Court, Infirmary Street
Leeds LS1 2JB
Contact: Ms R Connorton
Tel: 0113 243 0391
ruthconnorton@eversheds.co.uk

Eversheds
1 Callaghan Square
Cardiff CF10 1BT
Contact: Mrs H McNabb
Tel: 01222 471147
Heathermcnabb@eversheds.com

EXB Legal
10 Sandlea Park
West Kirby, Merseyside CH48 0QF
Contact: Elise Billy
Tel: 0151 6257217
Fax: 0870 1332884
law@exblegal.com

Field Fisher Waterhouse
35 Vine Street
London EC3N 2AA
Contact: Mr M Abell
Tel: 020 7861 4000
pma@ffwlaw.com

Hill Dickinson
Pearl Assurance House,
2 Derby Square
Liverpool L2 9XL
Tel: 0151 236 5400
Contact: Stephen Lansdown
Tel: 0151 243 2348
Fax: 0151 243 2301
stephen.lansdown@hilldickinson.com

HJ Walker Sibia Solicitors
603/614 The Cotton Exchange
Old Hall Street, Liverpool L3 9LQ
Contact: Mr G Howard Jones
Tel: 0151 227 2600
Fax: 0151 225 1551
law@hjws.com

Keeble Hawson
Protection House, 16–17 East Parade
Leeds LS1 2BR
Contact: Mr H D McKillop
Tel: 0113 244 3121
postroom@keeblehawson.co.uk

Leathes Prior
74 The Close
Norwich, Norfolk NR1 4DR
www.leathesprior.co.uk
Contact: Mr R J Chadd
Tel: 01603 610911
jchadd@leathesprior.co.uk

Levy & Mcrae
266 St Vincent Street
Glasgow G2 5RL
Contact: Mr A Caplan
Tel: 0141 307 2311
tonycaplan@lemac.co.uk

Maclay Murray & Spens
151 St Vincent Street
Glasgow G2 5NJ
www.maclaymurrayspens.co.uk
Contact: Ms M Burnside
Tel: 0141 2485011
mab@maclaymurrayspens.co.uk

Marshall Ross & Preveze
4 Fredricks Place
London EC2R 8AB
Contact: Mr R Levitt
Tel: 0207 3679000
Fax: 0207 3679004
r.levitt@mrp-law.co.uk

Mills and Reeve
54 Hagley Road
Edgbaston, Birmingham B16 8PE
Contact: Peter Manford
Tel: 0121 454 4000
Fax: 0121 456 3631

Mundays
Cedar House, 78 Portsmouth Road
Cobham, Surrey KT11 1AN
Contact: Nicola Broadhurst
Tel: 01932 590500
Fax: 01932 590220
nicola.broadhurst@mundays.co.uk

Nina Moran-Watson Solicitors
The Lodge House, Crow Lane
Tendring, Essex CO16 9AP
www.nmoran-watson.co.uk
Contact: Nina Moran-Watson
Tel: 0870 241 5092,
mobile 07968 445804
Fax: 0870 770 1623
nina@nmoran-watson.co.uk

Osborne Clarke
2 Temple Back East
Temple Quay, Bristol BS1 6EG
www.osborne-clarke.co.uk
Contact: Mr A Braithwaite
Tel: 0117 917 4178
andrew.braithwaite@osborneclarke.com

Owen White
Senate House, 62–70 Bath Road
Slough, Berks SL1 3SR
www.owenwhite.com
Contact: Anton Bates

Tel: 01753 536846
anton.bates@owenwhite.com

Parker Bullen
45 Castle Street
Salisbury, Wilts SP1 3SS
Contact: Mr M Lello
Tel: 01722 412000
Fax: 01722 411822
mark.lello@parkerbullen.com

Parker Bullen
8 Newbury Street
Andover, Hants SP10 1DW
Contact: Mr Chris Gwinn
Tel: 01264 400500
Fax: 01264 333686
chris.gwinn@parkerbullen.com

Paul K Nolan & Co
Merchants Hall,
25/26 Merchants Quay
Dublin 8, Ireland
Contact: Mr P Nolan
Tel: 01232 301933
marie@pkn.co.uk

Paul K Nolan & Co
135 Upper Lisburn Road
Belfast BT10 0LH
Contact: Mr P Nolan
Tel: 01232 301933
Fax: 01232 601784
marie@pkn.co.uk

Pinsents
3 Colmore Circus
Birmingham B4 6BH
www.pinsent-curtis.co.uk/expertise/
legalareas/busareas/franchise.htp
Contact: Mr J Pratt

Tel: 0121 200 1050
john.pratt@pinsent-curtis.co.uk

Shadbolt & Co
Chatham Court, Lesbourne
Reigate, Surrey RH2 7LD
www.shadboltlaw.co.uk
Contact: Caroline Abery
Tel: 01737 226277
Caroline_Abrey@Shadboltlaw.co.uk

Shakespeares Solicitors
Somerset House, Temple Street
Birmingham B2 5DJ
Contact: Jayne Lynn
Tel: 0121 632 4199
Fax: 0121 643 2257
jayne.lynn@shakespeares.co.uk

Sherrards
45 Grosvenor Road
St Albans AL1 3AW
Contact: Mr Manzoor Ishani
Tel: 01727 832 830
Fax: 01727 832 830
mgi@sherrards.co.uk

Sylvester Amiel Lewin & Horne
Pearl Assurance House,
319 Ballards Lane
London N12 8LY
Contact: Mr J Horne
Tel: 0181 446 4000
lawyers@sylvam.co.uk

Taylor Joynson Garrett
Carmelite, 50 Victoria Embankment
Blackfriars, London EC4Y 0DX
Contact: Mr C Lloyd
Tel: 0171 353 1234
clloyd@tjg.co.uk

Thomas Eggar
75 Shoe Lane
London EC4A 3JB
Contact: Richard Brown
Tel: 0207 8420000
Fax: 0207 8423900
richard.brown@thomaseggar.com

Thomas Eggar
Chatham Court, Lesbourne Road
Reigate, Surrey RH2 7FN
Contact: Mr M Crooks
Tel: 01737 240111
michael.crooks@thomaseggar.com

Thorntons WS
50 Castle Street
Dundee DD1 3RU
Contact: Stuart Brymer
Tel: 01382 229111
Fax: 01382 202288
dundee@thorntonsws.co.uk

TLT Solicitors
One Redcliffe Street
Bristol BS99 7JZ
www.TLTsolicitors.com
Contact: William Hull
Tel: 0117 9177777
Fax: 0117 9177778
whull@tltsolicitors.com

Wragge & Co
55 Colmore Row
Birmingham B3 2AS
Contact: Mr G D Harris
Tel: 0121 233 1000
michael_luckman@wragge.com

Wright Johnston & Mackenzie
302 St Vincent Street
Glasgow G2 5RZ
Contact: Clare Neilson
Tel: 0141 248 3434
Fax: 0141 221 1226
enquiries@wjm.co.uk

Business services

Thomson Directories
296 Farnborough Road
Farnborough, Hants GU14 7NU
Contact: Ms S Levey
Tel: 01252 390407
Fax: 01252 390402
john.antoniou@thomweb.co.uk

Yellow Pages
Directories House
50 Wellington Street
Slough, Berks SL1 1YL
Contact: Mr Richard Ashwood
Tel: 01753 553311
Fax: 01753 507285
richard.ashwood@yellowpages.co.uk

Exhibition organisers

Venture Marketing Group
Carlton Plaza,
111 Upper Richmond Road
Putney, London SW15 2TJ
Contact: Mr D Tuck
Tel: 020 8394 5230
david.tuck@vmgl.com

Financial services

Franchise Finance
105 Briar Avenue
Norbury, London SW16 3AG
Contact: Mr Nicholas Potter
Tel: 020 8679 0126
Fax: 020 8679 0126
potterpef@hotmail.com

Franchise manual publishing consultants

Manual Writers International
The Garden House
Norton Grange
Little Kineton, Warks CV35 0DP
www.manual-writers.com
Contact: Mrs Penny Hopkinson
Tel: 01926 641402
mob: 07956 315750
penny@manual-writers.com

Media & communications

Business Franchise Magazine
83–84 George Street
Richmond, Surrey TW9 1HE
Contact: Pat Malone
Tel: 020 8332 9995
editor@hdpublishing.co.uk

Daily Express
Ludgate House, 245 Blackfriars Road
London SE1 9UX
Contact: Chris Wield
Tel: 0207 922 2864
chris.wield@express.co.uk

Daily Mail
4th Floor, Northcliffe House,
2 Derry Street
Kensington, London W8 5TT
Contact: Steve Richardson
Tel: 0207 938 6433
Fax: 0207 937 7755
steve.richardson@dailymail.co.uk

Daltons Weekly
Link House, West Street
Poole, Dorset BH15 1LL UK
Tel: 020 8329 0150
Fax: 020 8329 0101
www.DaltonsBusiness.com
Contact: Mr Steve Croucher
Tel: 0208 3290279
steve.croucher@daltons.co.uk

The Franchise Magazine
Franchise House, 56 Surrey Street
Norwich NR3 1FD
Contact: Dr D R Chaplin
Tel: 01603 620301
enquiries@fdsltd.com

Franchise World
Highlands House, 165 The Broadway
Wimbledon, London SW19 1NE
Contact: Mr Robert Riding
Tel: 020 8605 2555
Fax: 020 8605 2556
info@franchiseworld.co.uk

The Mail on Sunday
2 Derry St, London W8 5TS
Contact: Peter Davenport
Tel: 020 7938 7331
peter.davenport@mailonsunday.co.uk

The Mirror
One Canada Square
Canary Wharf, London E14 5AP
Contact: Gareth Mortimer
Tel: 0207 293 3812
g.williams@mgn.co.uk

The Scotsman Publications
108 Holyrood Road, Edinburgh
EH8 8AS
Contact: Mr R Shepherd
Tel: 0131 620 8620
rshepherd@scotsman.com

whichfranchise.com
78 Carlton Place, Glasgow G5 9TH
www.whichfranchise.com
Contact: Mr J Sellyn
Tel: 0141 429 5900
info@whichfranchise.com

Bankers

Bank of Scotland
High Street
Purley, Surrey CR8 2AF
Contact: Mark Pavis
Tel: 0845 300 1686
Fax: 0208 763 9061
franchising@bankofscotland.co.uk

HSBC
Franchise Unit, 24th Floor
8 Canada Square, London E14 5HQ
www.ukbusiness.hsbc.com
Contact: Cathryn Hayes
Tel: 020 7992 1062
Fax: 020 7991 4604
franchiseunit@hsbc.com

Lloyds TSB
Business Banking
Canon's House, PO Box 112
Canon's Way, Bristol BS99 7LB
www.lloydstsbbusiness.co.uk/
Contact: Alick Jones
Tel: 0117 943 3089
franchising@lloydstsb.co.uk

NatWest UK
Natwest Franchise Section
Level 2, Waterhouse Square
138–140 Holborn, London
EC1N 2TH
Tel: 020 7427 8405
www.natwest.com
Contact: Mark Scott
Tel: 020 7427 8405
franchise.retailbanking@natwest.com

The Royal Bank of Scotland
Franchise Department
PO Box 20000, The Younger Building
Drummond House,
3 Redheughs Avenue
Edinburgh EH12 9RB
www.rbs.co.uk/franchise/
Contact: Alan Smart
Tel: 0131 5232178
Fax: 0131 5235183
alan.smart@rbs.co.uk

Chartered accountants

Beresfords
Castle House, Castle Hill Avenue
Folkestone, Kent CT20 2TQ
Contact: Mr T C Hindle
Tel: 01303 850992
Fax: 01303 850979
mail@beresfordsaccountants.com

Morris & Co
Ashton House, Chadwick Street
Moreton, Wirral CH46 7TE
www.moco.co.uk
Contact: Phil Harrison
Tel: 0151 678 7979
Fax: 0151 606 0909
franchise@moco.co.uk

Rees Pollock
7 Pilgrim Street
London EC4V 6DR
www.reespollock.co.uk
Contact: Robin Harding
Tel: 020 7329 6404
robin@reespollock.co.uk

WDM Associates
Oakfield House, 378 Brandon Street
Motherwell ML1 1XA
Contact: Mr Terry Dunne
Tel: 01698 250251
Fax: 01698 250261
terry@wdmassocs.co.uk

Development agencies

Scottish Enterprise
150 Broomielaw, Atlantic Quay
Glasgow G2 8LU
Contact: Mr Brian Smail
Tel: 0141 228 2730
Fax: 0141 228 2559
brian.smail@scotent.co.uk

Scottish Enterprise Glasgow
Atrium Court, 50 Waterloo Street
Glasgow G2 6HQ
Contact: Mr Bill Cook
Tel: 0141 2428236
Fax: 0141 2428322
bill.cook@scotent.co.uk

Franchise consultants

AMO Consulting
74 Kirk Street
Strathaven ML10 6BA
www.amoconsulting.com
Contact: Mr Euan Fraser
Tel: 01357 523308
Fax: 01357 523308
euanfraser@bun.com

BDO Stoy Hayward
8 Baker Street, London W1U 3LL
www.mchardy.biz
Contact: Max McHardy
Tel: 0207 486 5888
max.mchardy@bdo.co.uk

David Acheson Partnership
14 Royena Place, Marcus Beach
Queensland 4573, Australia
Contact: David Acheson
Tel: 00 61 074 481 774
Fax: 00 61 074 481 775

FDS Midlands
28 Footherley Road
Shenstone, Lichfield, Staffs WS14 0NJ
Tel: 01543 483509
Fax: 01543 481029
Contact: Ken Young
Tel: 01543 483509
Fax: 01543 481029
fdsmids@supanet.com

Franchise Company
Ashburn House, 84 Grange Road
Darlington, Co Durham DL1 5NP
www.franchisecompany.co.uk
Contact: Ken Rostron
Tel: 01325 251455
Fax: 01325 251466
info@franchisecompany.co.uk

Franchise Development Services
Franchise House, 56 Surrey Street
Norwich, NR1 3FD
www.franchise-group.com
Contact: Mr P Hague
Tel: 01603 620301
enquiries@fdsltd.com

Franchise Development Services (Middle East)
PO Box 221
Jeddah 21411, Saudi Arabia
Contact: Mr Talai Badkook
Tel: 00 996 2 651 5123
Fax: 00 996 2 651 5123

Franchise Development Services (Northern)
Suite 19, Oakfield House,
Oakfield Road
Altrincham, Cheshire WA15 8EW
Tel: 0161 926 9882
Fax: 0161 926 8257
Contact: Tony Urwin
Tel: 0161 9269882
Fax: 0161 9268257
info@fdsnorthern.com

Franchise Development Services (Southern)
Maple Grove, Bradfield
Reading, Berks RG7 6DH
Contact: Gordon Patterson
Tel: 01189 745115
Fax: 0118 974 4018
franchising@fdssouthern.com

Franchise Development Services (Taiwan)
6F-1 Jen Ai Road, Section 4
Taipei, Taiwan
Contact: Victor Tan
Tel: 00 886 2 755 4021
Fax: 00 886 2 755 1243

Franchise Options
56 Carters Close, Sherington
Newport Pagnell, Bucks MK16 9NW
Contact: Paul Tough
Tel: 01908 616300
Fax: 01908 616300
paultough@franchiseoptions.co.uk

Franchise Your Business
Bywood, Arbrook Lane
Esher, Surrey KT10 9EG
www.franchiseyourbusiness.co.uk
Tel: 01372 470010
info@franchiseyourbusiness.co.uk

Horwath Franchising
25 New Steet Square
London EC4A 3LN
www.horwathfranchising.co.uk
Contact: Brian Duckett
Tel: 020 7 917 9824
sarah@horwathfranchising.co.uk

Horwath Franchising
Keeper's Cottage, 8 Manor Road
Cossington, Somerset TA7 8JR
www.horwathfranchising.co.uk
Contact: Paul Monaghan
Tel: 01278 723625
paul@horwathfranchising.co.uk

Horwath Franchising
Innovation Centre, Innovation Way
York Science Park, York YO10 5DG
Tel: 01904 561598
www.horwathfranchising.co.uk
Contact: Mr Bill Pegram
Tel: 01904 561598
mobile 07968 167422
bill@horwathfranchising.co.uk

Peter Williams
40 Newquay Close
Nuneaton, Warks CV11 6FH
Contact: Mr Peter Williams
Tel: 02476 329260
Fax: 02476 329260
peter.williams@franchise-consult.fsnet.co.uk

Recruitment consultants

MRI Worldwide
15 Wheeler Gate, Nottingham
NG1 2NA
Contact: Kate Stojko
Tel: 0115 852 4040
Fax: 0115 852 4001
enquiries@carnellrecruitment.co.uk

Training providers

The Franchise Training Centre
25 New Street Square, London
EC4A 3LN
www.horwathfranchising.co.uk
Contact: Mr B Duckett
Tel: 020 7917 9824
sarah@horwathfranchising.co.uk

Appendix IV

Useful Web sites

www.british-franchising.org
www.britishfranchisedirectory.com
www.findafranchise.co.uk
www.franchisebusiness.co.uk
www.franchiseconcepts.co.uk
www.franchisedirect.com
www.franchise-group.com
www.franchiseopportunities.com
www.franchisesales.com
www.FranchiseSolutions.com
www.franchiseworld.co.uk
www.franinfo.co.uk
www.360franchising.co.uk

Index of advertisers

Domino's	v
Kall Kwik	ix
Netspace	xxii–xxiv
Rainbow International	xxi
RE/MAX	xi–xiii
Snackpoint Ltd	xv–xvii
SprayAway	xviii–xix